Corporate Social Responsibility and the Inclusivity of Women in the Mining Industry:

Emerging Research and Opportunities

Nattavud Pimpa
Mahidol University, Thailand

Timothy Moore
The University of Melbourne, Australia

A volume in the Advances in
Business Strategy and Competitive
Advantage (ABSCA) Book Series

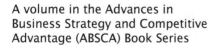

Published in the United States of America by
IGI Global
Business Science Reference (an imprint of IGI Global)
701 E. Chocolate Avenue
Hershey PA, USA 17033
Tel: 717-533-8845
Fax: 717-533-8661
E-mail: cust@igi-global.com
Web site: http://www.igi-global.com

Library of Congress Cataloging-in-Publication Data

Names: Pimpa, Nattavud, 1974- author. I Moore, Timothy, 1960- author.
Title: Corporate social responsibility and the inclusivity of women in the
   mining industry : emerging research and opportunities / by Nattavud Pimpa
   and Timothy Moore.
Description: Hershey : Business Science Reference, [2017]
Identifiers: LCCN 2017022434I ISBN 9781522538110 (hardcover) I ISBN
   9781522538127 (ebook)
Subjects: LCSH: Mineral industries--Laos. I Mineral industries--Thailand. I
   Women miners--Laos--Economic conditions. I Women
   miners--Thailand--Economic conditions. I Women's rights--Laos. I Women's
   rights--Thailand. I Social responsibility of business--Laos. I Social
   responsibility of business--Thailand.
Classification: LCC HD8700.4 .P56 2017 I DDC 331.4/8220959.--dc23 LC record available at
https://lccn.loc.gov/2017022434

This book is published in the IGI Global book series Advances in Business Strategy and
Competitive Advantage (ABSCA) (ISSN: 2327-3429; eISSN: 2327-3437)

British Cataloguing in Publication Data
A Cataloguing in Publication record for this book is available from the British Library.

All work contributed to this book is new, previously-unpublished material.
The views expressed in this book are those of the authors, but not necessarily of the publisher.

For electronic access to this publication, please contact: eresources@igi-global.com.

Advances in Business Strategy and Competitive Advantage (ABSCA) Book Series

ISSN:2327-3429
EISSN:2327-3437

Editor-in-Chief: Patricia Ordóñez de Pablos, Universidad de Oviedo, Spain

MISSION

Business entities are constantly seeking new ways through which to gain advantage over their competitors and strengthen their position within the business environment. With competition at an all-time high due to technological advancements allowing for competition on a global scale, firms continue to seek new ways through which to improve and strengthen their business processes, procedures, and profitability.

The **Advances in Business Strategy and Competitive Advantage (ABSCA) Book Series** is a timely series responding to the high demand for state-of-the-art research on how business strategies are created, implemented and re-designed to meet the demands of globalized competitive markets. With a focus on local and global challenges, business opportunities and the needs of society, the **ABSCA** encourages scientific discourse on doing business and managing information technologies for the creation of sustainable competitive advantage.

COVERAGE

- Entrepreneurship & Innovation
- Joint Ventures
- Value Chain
- Strategic Management
- Balanced Scorecard
- Outsourcing
- Customer-Orientation Strategy
- International Business Strategy
- Ethics and Business Strategy
- Core Competencies

IGI Global is currently accepting manuscripts for publication within this series. To submit a proposal for a volume in this series, please contact our Acquisition Editors at Acquisitions@igi-global.com or visit: http://www.igi-global.com/publish/.

Titles in this Series

For a list of additional titles in this series, please visit:
https://www.igi-global.com/book-series/advances-business-strategy-competitive-advantage/73672

For an entire list of titles in this series, please visit:
https://www.igi-global.com/book-series/advances-business-strategy-competitive-advantage/73672

701 East Chocolate Avenue, Hershey, PA 17033, USA
Tel: 717-533-8845 x100 • Fax: 717-533-8661
E-Mail: cust@igi-global.com • www.igi-global.com

Table of Contents

Preface

This book emanates from our passion for gender and business issues. Modern business organisations actively promote equity and well-being in the host countries where they operate. Most firms understand that corporate social responsibility (CSR) focusing on women and girls can promote relationships among the firm, the community and various other stakeholders. We focus on the mining industry in Mekong countries because we have learnt from a number of communities in the region that the mining industry influences the life of the people.

For years, scholars and practitioners in various disciplines have argued for and against the concept of mining and development. CSR for women is debatable by all stakeholders in the international mining industry. In fact, the debate on CSR by the mining industry in developing countries is polarised. In the context of the extractive industries, its impact is seen as significant or negligible, depending on the party and the expectations. Mining companies themselves have presented a range of arguments in support of the case for CSR for women in the extractive industries. As indicated, these include—but are not limited to—benefits of making a business case for CSR, companies needing a 'social licence to operate' and stakeholders holding management accountable.

We started this project in 2013, in order to explore how multinational mining corporations influence the life of women in the mining communities of Laos and Thailand. The project started from a simple question: What are the relationships among mining industry growth, gender equality, and national factors? We hoped to understand ways to improve living conditions and the economic situation in the host countries of multinational mining corporations.

At an early stage of this project, we met with delegates from three mining companies in both countries, examined their ideas and actions, and explored theories from the government and business organisations related to their social responsibility to the local community.

Scholars in business and community development commonly refer to concepts such as 'corporate social responsibility', 'corporate citizenship' or 'corporate stewardship'. From 2014 to 2016, we visited three mining communities in Laos and Thailand and got to know various members of each community. Most of them are women who play different roles in the community. Interestingly, we learnt a great deal about socioeconomic factors influencing the livelihood of the community. All mining companies with which we worked for this project increasingly signal to their stakeholders in local and international communities that they are responding to the imperative for more sustainable approaches. Hence, CSR for women is no longer just an option, but comprises core policies for most mining companies.

In fact, we realise that CSR is far more contentious in the case of the international mining industry in developing countries. The industry has heavily popularised CSR and continues to do so. They may struggle to prove the impact of their CSR programmes. Nonetheless, they still must continue their social-responsibility activities with the community.

Specifically, it is unclear what function CSR, clearly a Western construct, plays in such settings and societal contexts. In developing countries such as Laos and Thailand, comprehensive environmental regulations are in place, alongside labour unions, media, NGOs and a wealth of consumer demands. The insinuation is that these elements generate 'invisible' pressures that drive mining multinational corporations (MNCs) to adopt voluntary CSR practises, presumably analogous to the way in which the 'invisible hand' regulates the marketplace. But what is the CSR story in developing countries? What can they do to improve quality of life among diverse groups in the community?

We aim to capture various dimensions of mining MNCs and development aspects in Laos and Thailand, particularly from women's perspectives. We present project process and findings in this book as contributions to understanding business, gender and society.

The project is funded by the Australian Department of Foreign Affairs and Trade (DFAT) through the AusAID Development Research Awards Scheme (ADRAS). Our team thanks DFAT for their financial and technical support while we were working in Laos, Thailand and Australia.

The project would have been impossible without support from the local communities of Vilabouly (in Savannakhet, Laos) and Tab Klor (Pijit-Petchaboon in Thailand). All participants, community leaders, and particularly women have been supportive in the process of data collection in both countries. Supports from the Women Union of Vilabouly, the National University of Laos, and Mahidol University were tremendous. We sincerely thank all of you.

For technical support and links to the community, we thank Luke Stephens and his team from MMG company in Laos, and Sirirat Schmidt and her team from Akara Resources in Thailand.

Nattavud Pimpa
Mahidol University, Thailand

Timothy Moore
The University of Melbourne, Australia

Introduction

We present this book in the form of research insight, where we focus our key points on how the mining industry influences the life of women through CSR programmes. We are aware of the discursive masculinity and femininity of mining from gender and feminist studies. We still integrate concepts from gender studies, business and management, and community studies into our study. Hence, the book is multidisciplinary in nature.

The general message of the project is a hopeful one; the relationship between mining multinational corporations (MNCs) and local communities is undergoing a largely positive evolution. More importantly, very practical programmes and policies from mining MNCs can be implemented to increase the probability of positive experiences among women and girls in the host countries.

After working on this project with key stakeholders in international mining in Laos and Thailand, we realise that in many natural-resource-rich locations in rural Southeast Asia, development of these resources, especially through mining, is becoming the dominant economic activity and source of employment for men and women. It is truly influential for the community. In this regard, discrimination against women in the workplace and the wider community means they often are grossly underrepresented in this new economic activity. It is important to elucidate factors underlying this condition, in order to enhance gender inclusiveness and, ultimately, community economic development.

Recently, questions have arisen around how mining MNCs relate to their communities and the broader society. Therefore, mining MNCs have a responsibility to society that goes beyond making profits and should extend to issues of general concern to the society in which they operate. Empowering women through their economic activities such as employment, income generation programmes, educational development and other CSR activities must be carefully planned and executed.

If employment by mining companies is a significant way to empower women in Lao PDR and Thailand, unknowns remain in the mining-industry context:

- What approach should be taken to providing decent and equitable employment for women?
- To what extent can mining MNCs utilise their resources and capabilities to empower women in the community?

This gap in knowledge is an alarming issue. In order to understand these points, this project focuses on investigating this issue. Key findings could impact upon the action of local governments, as well as the mining industry in Lao PDR and Thailand.

Chapter 1
Mining Industry and Its Influence

ABSTRACT

The mining industry has tremendous impact on people and communities. The opening of a large mine has economic, environmental, and social consequences at the national, state, or provincial and local levels. Mining company activities can also positively and negatively influence many lives. The challenge is for mining multinational corporations (MNCs), communities, and governments to rationalise real action for the community. As initiatives and programmes show success, these experiences can be woven into ongoing operations if lines of communication are kept open. Mining MNCs can promote dialogue among the various stakeholders and disseminate the results of efforts that have helped enhance the sustainability of the economic impacts of mining. This chapter discusses various impacts of the mining industry on women, including skill development, poverty, health, and economic impacts. Issues of corporate social responsibility as a key function of mining MNCs in Thailand and Laos are discussed.

DOI: 10.4018/978-1-5225-3811-0.ch001

INTRODUCTION

Corporate Social Responsibility (CSR) refers to voluntary actions undertaken by mining companies to either improve the living conditions (economic, social, environmental) of local communities or to reduce the negative impacts of mining projects. (DFAT, 2014)

The mining industry has considerable potential to help reduce poverty and accelerate human development through the promotion of gender equity, increasing government and community revenues and generating employment among women in the community. This industry has been a central socioeconomic activity in many communities worldwide. Most of them are in emerging and frontier economies.

While ideologies of human rights, gender equity and the elimination of discrimination underpin most large multinational corporations' (MNCs) employment policies, counter-ideologies of gender equity often prevail in practise (Moon, 2008). Most mining MNCs have been striving to adopt business ideologies and developmental practises that promote equity between men and women. However, women in the mining industry reportedly still struggle to work at a similar level to men (Mercier & Gier, 2007).

However, management of mining impacts in developing countries can be complex and challenging for all stakeholders. Extraction of natural resources through activities such as mining is limited to a particular geographical area. Often its activities are conducted in or near communities and have direct or indirect impacts on community resources, capabilities and well-being, thus leading to a state of poverty, violent behavior, and resentment by communities toward these businesses, and creating other forms of human deprivation such as water and air pollution, and issues of land access, farming and toxicity.

Previous studies (Yakovleva & Vazquez-Brust, 2012; Oxfam, 2009) also confirm that several factors can be attributed to gender disengagement practises among stakeholders in the mining industry including mining MNCs, local authorities, communities, NGOs and local government agencies. The failure to promote engagement among these stakeholders and existing unstable and weak national institutions leads to gender-based disadvantages (DeSoto, 2000).

Whilst there is evidence of increasingly effective and sophisticated developmental activities on gender equity by mining MNCs, there is no clear understanding of various approaches they have adopted. Due to their significant economic and social roles, we must understand how mining MNCs promote gender equity and integrate women into their operations. More importantly, factors promoting women in international business organisations (such as mining MNCs) must be comprehended in order to support long-term strategies to empower and promote women in this male-dominated industry.

As gender equity in international business is a salient issue, it has been rather difficult for mining MNCs to claim lack of awareness of their contributions in this area. However, this has not led to constraints on mining MNCs to behave according to norms that would be conducive to mitigating this important issue in their host and home countries.

WOMEN AND MINING: GENDER AND CULTURAL PERSPECTIVES

Mining has long been a male-dominated industry in which women continue to be underrepresented in leadership positions. In order to achieve substantive gender equality and the economic benefits of women in leadership roles, we must understand how to increase the representation of women and strengthen the pipeline of female talent in the mining industry, particularly in developing countries.

According to Oxfam (2009), women's needs and opportunities are often overlooked in the extractives industry, leading to disproportionate negative impacts such as family and social disruption, environmental degradation, loss of employment and risks to security and well-being. Historically, women working in mining are excluded from the extractives value chain, deprived of opportunities and benefits generally developed in that context. If not addressed, these factors could further widen the gender gaps in access to resources and resource-related opportunities.

Male-dominated culture also structures the day-to-day work and job design in large-scale mines. For instance, mining is performed in routinely long hours of work that severely limit part-time or flexible work practises for workers to integrate and balance their work and personal or family life. Where there are flexible work practises available, there is limited engagement, so the full-time work week is the norm. This is a key barrier to workers with both caregiving and earning responsibilities, predominantly women. The culture of a male breadwinner or an 'ideal worker' norm underpins mining culture and, despite flexible work initiatives and gender-diversity strategies, appears to be pervasive in many locations.

Women are impacted by mining in all aspects of life and in all stages of the lifecycle. They are the key to reversing the disadvantages faced not only by them but also by their communities. Hiring women has been shown to have a greater welfare impact on families than hiring men. In addition, women spend income differently than men do. In comparison to men, where women control the family income, child health and wellbeing have been shown to improve. Therefore, investing in the health and wellbeing of women and increasing opportunities for women in the mining workforce and the community can provide a basis for sound economic and human rights policy.

The Workplace Gender Equality Agency (2013) reveals that the percentage of women in the global mining industry has increased from 12.6% in 2004-2005 to 17.0% in 2011-2012. However, it is still the second most male-dominated industry, behind the construction industry.

The ideology of the male breadwinner in the mining industry and the reputed toughness of the work that disqualifies women from mining often disintegrate when operations expand or the supply of labour shrinks, when men require family assistance in the mines or when these 'masculine' jobs became seasonal and low-paid (Mercier & Gier, 2007). In fact, as recent research in business and gender reveals, women often moved into the diggings and even dominated mining where enterprises were fairly marginal, or provided sustenance when men were required or chose to work elsewhere (Mercier & Gier, 2007; Kemp & Owen, 2013).

Previous studies (Pattenden, 1998; Sharma & Kiran; 2013) show that women can be allowed underground as independent wage earners, or to assist men (fathers and husbands) in the mining industry. For the most part, however, Mercier and Gier (2007) find that mining became more exclusively associated with men as it became more capitalised and centralised. Concentrated urban, industrial sites typically insisted on a rigid sexual division of labour, but more rural and subsidiary operations involved families or became the domain of women's work.

Pattenden (1998) proposed that for women, in particular, extractive industries can provide opportunities for a better life, including increased employment opportunities, access to revenue and expanded investment in the local community. Women-led businesses can flourish in the extractives supply chain. Working with and investing in women also makes good business sense—for example, many companies are recruiting women to drive trucks and operate machinery, often finding that women employees achieve an impressive safety record and reduced maintenance of equipment.

Too often, however, these opportunities do not materialise and extractive industries deliver as much or more damage than benefit. Achieving the development gains that extractive industries promise, in particular for women, depends on understanding and managing that risk.

Sexist views faced by women entering the mining workforce often limit career advancement (Dutta, 2008). For instance, a feminist reconsideration of mining would carefully handle the literature relating to the 'impacts of mining on women and their careers'. Some of this literature has helped give rise to the stereotypes of women as victims; for example, 'the prostitute' who introduces or spreads HIV/AIDS, or the 'contract wife' who provides concrete evidence of the fallen status of women (Lahiri-Dutt, 2011).

These are significant management issues that mining MNCs must understand in order to find ways to mitigate management risks and improve work conditions. Studies in mining and gender confirm that masculine norms sustain structural barriers that marginalise and negatively impact women in household, community and employment relations (Bose, 2004).

Issues on gender equity in Laos are not that dissimilar from most other countries in the Mekong region. In Laos, women and girls living in rural and remote areas of Laos are often the most disadvantaged. Men are usually described as the heads of households, representing their families at official meetings (Oxfam, 2017). Many women are illiterate and do not speak the national language used for education (La Shrestha, 2010). Prevailing social and cultural norms mean women are not sufficiently confident to give their opinions, and do not demonstrate simple meeting skills such as taking turns to speak out. Therefore, often women cannot participate fully in village development activity processes (Oxfam, 2017).

From gender perspectives, Moretti (2006) suggested that despite the acknowledgment of complementary and symmetrical gender relations, researchers depict mining as an exceptionally masculinised industry in terms of the composition of its workforce and its cultures of production, as well as its symbolic exploitation of feminised nature.

It is evident that mining 'is so "naturally" masculine [that] its gender effects are invisible' (Oxfam, 2017). Until the beginning of the 21st century, studies on mining neglected to focus on gender and the social position of women as workers, providers and wives. Current research on gender and mining asserts that women's land rights and their rights to representation within the mining community are commonly diminished in the context of mining activities.

How far mining MNCs have gone when it comes to business and organisational strategies to empower women remains unclear. The gap between the rhetoric and the reality of gender and diversity-management issues occurs through the assumption that complexity might only be reduced by power structures in organisations—and conversely, gender and diversity in the international mining industry will be able to unfold by changing these power relations.

MINING MNCS AND CSR

CSR in mining tends to be defined narrowly to only mean MNC-implemented community development programmes, rather than also encompassing concepts of corporate citizenship, labour, human rights and the environment.

Mining companies have been challenged over social issues such as human rights violations, environmental problems, corruption scandals and tailings-dam accidents, triggering the emergence of anti-mining NGOs that have questioned the sector's ability to behave sustainably (Werthmann, 2009). Global mining MNCs have come under intense pressure and scrutiny from environmental agencies, NGOs, indigenous people and human-rights movements formed in response to concerns about the social and environmental impacts of mining operations (Visser, 2010)

Also, often excluded from company discourses on CSR as a success are questions of effectiveness that have long been debated within development theory (Merino & Valor, 2011), and further questions of whether mining companies can successfully act in the same ways as other development agencies. To what extent are companies in control of setting their CSR policies and programmes? Are they structurally able to perform as a development agency? Is sustainable development possible given the finite nature of mineral resources and eventual mine closure?

As addressed by Lauwo (2018), over the last decade an increasing number of studies have investigated gender-related issues in the mining sectors, but most have focused on addressing the dilemmas facing women in small-scale and artisanal mining. Campbell (2012, p. 138) maintains that contrary to an initial statement that foreign investments from large mining MNCs were much needed in the mining sector, fully justifying the negative impacts that were to be mitigated by voluntary measures, there is increasing evidence of deplorable social and environmental impacts of mining activities in developing countries.

Due to the regulations and social requirements of host countries, CSR has become a common language championed by large mining companies. The concept of mining and their CSR revolves around notions of ethics, transparency, accountability and responsible practises. The pressure to embrace CSR is far greater in the extractive industries because the industrial-scale extraction of natural resources affects both the environment and local populations (Lauwo, 2018). Therefore, in the last decades, we have witnessed the growth of CSR strategies and activities by mining MNCs. Arguably, due to the impact of the mining industry, mining MNCs will need to carefully and continuously implement their relationship with the community. Beyond financial benefits and taxation, CSR has long been seen as an important business element for mining MNCs.

One of the first and most fundamental issues concerning the approach of mining companies worldwide to CSR is their formal regulation. This is important to ensuring that transparent and ethical behaviour are consistent with the organisation and practised in its relationships. Obviously, a comprehensive approach to these issues by the company ensures that it has a separate CSR strategy (Majer, 2013).

CSR refers to the relationship between business and society, where the role of business is purported to go beyond the provision of goods and services (Donaldson & Preston, 1995) The traditional neoclassical view of business, the cornerstone of capitalism, is that the role of business is to create and protect shareholder value, thereby driving economic and social development through profit maximisation.

Made famous by neoliberals such as Milton Friedman, this dominant view of business as contributing to society through wealth generation is contested by those who argue that business must take on an expanded role in society in light of the increasing privatisation of social and welfare services, and the diminishing role of the state. Following the end of the Cold War, firms stepped into this vacuum and, enabled by globalisation, were able to accrue growing power and influence over global markets.

Entering the 21st century, MNCs made up over half of the world's 100 largest economies. Walmart's sales alone in 2007 eclipsed the economies of 114 countries (Werbach, 2009). CSR proponents argue that with this power comes responsibility. Elkington (1998) also argues that:

Environmental reporting is now well established, as of course is financial reporting. But further challenges lie ahead for companies looking to evaluate social indicators in such areas as community, employee and supplier

7

relationships. The pressure for accountability, together with the significant expense of producing the data, will develop powerful pressures towards the integration of financial, social and environmental accounting and reporting…

Companies, and their stakeholders, will have no option but to address this emerging 'triple bottom line'. They will have to work harder to assess what really matters to them and which indicators will be seen by key stakeholders. (Elkington, 1998 pp-124)

Caroll (1979) conceptualises CSR as a four-part definition that can be visually represented by a four-tiered pyramid of business responsibilities—economic, legal, ethical and voluntary or philanthropic (Carroll, 1979). The pyramid is founded upon the economic responsibilities of a business, as a basis for all other additional activities to occur, with legal, ethical and philanthropic tiers layered upward. Carroll notes that this is not a sequential process; rather, all these activities occur at once in a firm that is committed to CSR. These four domains underpin Eisendhart's (1998) related definition of the triple bottom line where, drawing upon conventional bottom-line accounting as a metaphor, he advocates for the integration of a firm's social and environmental impact into its bottom line to capture a more accurate picture of its overall corporate performance (Eisendhart, 1998).

While Carroll's classical definition, first coined in the late 1970s, provided the basis for the empirical research around CSR and corporate social performance, in the 1980s and 1990s the focus was on understanding how to measure and operationalise CSR. The proliferation of CSR studies gave way to attendant theories of stakeholder and management theory, business ethics, corporate social performance and corporate citizenship that used CSR as their base but placed these different concepts at the centre of their investigations (Carroll 1979).

More recently, Schwab (2008) defines CSR as a suite of activities centering around corporate responsibility. He opposes the use of CSR as the catchall term to describe what he considers five distinct corporate-engagement activities (corporate governance, corporate philanthropy, corporate social entrepreneurship, CSR, corporate citizenship), and advocates for the currency of the term '*corporate citizenship*' as a holistic realisation of all these activities.

In Schwab's (2008) view, CSR is programmatic in focus and often associated with time-bound incremental initiatives impacting directly on a firm's operations. This narrow focus on the immediate activities of the firm at the micro level are part of the reason why global social challenges such as climate change and poverty persist, despite the proliferation of CSR initiatives.

More specifically, the European Union (EU) also has been contributing to the universal debate on CSR, providing an analysis of CSR as 'a concept whereby companies/business firms decide voluntarily to contribute to the betterment of the social world and uplifting of society and a cleaner environment' (Sharma & Kiran, 2013).

In contrast, corporate citizenship is concerned with taking a macro view of social problems and manifests through thought leadership and advocacy in the global arena. Corporate citizenship recognises that MNCs operate in a global space that is not governed by one set of laws and therefore cannot be influenced by any one government.

International cooperation between governments, international organisations and transnational civil society are necessary to overcome these global challenges, which is in a company's interest as it relies on global development, stability and increased prosperity to operate.

Arguments for an expanded social role for business call for decisive action on sustainability issues that are often global in scope, complex in nature and beyond the jurisdiction of any one government or set of laws. It is therefore unsurprising that CSR is highly contested and can be met with resistance by the private sector, which seeks to clearly define and, in some cases, constrain the scope of its role in addressing complex social challenges that may not always prove profitable (Waddock, 2005).

Social action is inherently political, and the contested nature of CSR means that companies understand their social responsibilities to varying degrees, depending on a diverse range of factors such as sector, regulatory environment, organisational structure, leadership and political will. Consequently, there is no one fixed definition nor agreed-upon response to CSR (Suchman, 1995)

An Australian inquiry conducted by the Parliamentary Joint Committee on Financial Services in fical year 2006 emphasised that 'because of the sheer diversity of modern corporations—in terms of size, sectors, stakeholder structures and strategies—the concept of corporate responsibility can have a different meaning to different people and different organisations. The CSR lexicon is constantly contested and shifting, which can obscure the meaning of social responsibility or seek to reframe it in more manageable terms. The CSR discourse itself, supposedly oriented around social change, can be used to contain rather than engender it, by creating confusion about how to manifest this change beyond the capitalist paradigm and without challenging the primacy of markets and corporations as their key agents (Ganesh, 2007).

THE ROLE OF MINING MULTINATIONAL CORPORATIONS

The end of the Cold War precipitated a growing acknowledgement of the social role of business. A new social contract was forged between the state and the private sector as globalisation heralded the ascent of free-market values. Traditional social services formerly managed by government were privatised and given over to business, based on a neoliberal rationale of greater efficiency (Capaldi, 2005). No longer was the state the primary provider of social services; the private sector, with its increasing market share and influence, was increasingly impinging on government as the most powerful social institution.

The diminishing role of the state coupled with the advent of globalisation meant that 'the institution that stepped into that vacuum of social responsibility was the modern business organisation' (McMillan, 2007, p. 15).

Debates in the 1990s around CSR became concerned with dealing with the fallout from neoliberalism and profound effects of the globalisation process. However, the expansion of the private sector's social role was met with opposition, as many neoliberals claimed that the traditional role of business was strictly to deliver returns to shareholders.

This neoclassical view was espoused most prominently by the economist Milton Friedman, who famously wrote, 'there is one and only one social responsibility of business—to use its resources and engage in activities designed to increase its profits so long as it stays within the rules of the game' (Friedman, 1970, p. 6). His view for business is only to engage in open and free competition without deception or fraud. In sum, he proposed to the public that corporations are a species of private property and, consequently, they have exactly the same social responsibility as other businesses in a capitalist economy—that is, to make as much money as possible, so long as they stay within the rules of the game, which is to say, engaging in open and free competition.

Although Friedman's wholesale rejection of the social role of business is less common, there is contrasting opinion within the private sector about what social responsibilities exist and how to act upon them, let alone how much action should take place.

Actors in the private sector, such as mining MNCs, are increasingly aware of community expectations surrounding their corporate behaviour. Stakeholder theory holds that shareholders are not the primary audience to which business must be accountable, but rather a wider range of actors who are impacted by the firm or have an interest in its activities (Donaldson & Preston, 1995). Employees, customers, suppliers and the community grant the business its social licence to operate, as firms draw on communal resources such as good health and education systems, clean air and water, adequate housing, strong families and community harmony.

According to legitimacy theory, firms have no automatic right to exist or consume communal resources. Where they abuse these resources through environmental degradation or anti-human-rights practises, for example, the community may withdraw its social licence to operate (Deegan, 2002).

Social legitimacy is ongoing and must be maintained through inclusive community practises and by staying in touch with stakeholder opinions and expectations. Businesses that lose their social licence to operate have often done so through large-scale media scandals and must often make amends with the general public, as exemplified by the collapse of Enron in 2002 or, more recently, BP's Gulf of Mexico oil-spill disaster. These firms suffer plummeting share prices, loss of goodwill and reputational value that translates into reduced sales and profits, thereby building a compelling business case for action on corporate sustainability.

Historically, MNCs in developing countries have acted on their social responsibilities to varying degrees. Several high-profile corporate scandals in less developed countries (LDCs), such as the Nigerian Brent Spar incident in 1995 and the Nike sweatshop protests in the late 1990s, prompted growing global awareness of corporate irresponsibilities. Transnational civil-society networks applied pressure to MNCs operating in LDCs. Aided by information and communication technologies that facilitated the sharing of information and innovative forms of community organisation, companies were called to account for their practises in the global South. The resource-extractive sector in particular was scrutinised for its role in environmentally and socially exploitative practises (Lynch, 2002). Companies such as Rio Tinto and BHP Billiton were criticised for their role in displacing indigenous communities and causing conflict, which in some instances incited violence and gross human-rights violations. For more globalised MNCs operating in the South from their northern headquarters, CSR became a programmatic response to this transnational criticism.

While CSR is characterised as an opportunity for MNCs to deliver more efficient solutions for public goods and services previously provided by the state, particularly in the South where the state can be less robust, critics argue that this has exacerbated unequal power structures between developed countries and LDCs. Globally, 'the increased reliance on corporate actors in the provision of societal goals might also create or reinforce a global governance regime that has repeatedly been characterised as 'neo-colonialist' (Barkemeyer, 2009). According to the UN Global Compact (2013), the role of MNCs in development lies in their potential to address social challenges through global partnerships and cooperation. However, the achievement of the Millennium Development Goals (MDGs), which map out eight key goals in poverty alleviation, look to fall short, and many of the issues not only persist—if anything, they have become worse. Some have questioned the CSR agenda itself, which is largely reflective of northern values and is predicated on a bias for voluntary mechanisms and a structural framework of robust social institutions, such as rule of law and an independent media. Others have pointed to the persistence of global inequalities and have called for the reconceptualisation of CSR as oriented more explicitly toward global corporate citizenship and adopting a macro-level perspective, as opposed to a narrow view of CSR that comprises local programmes and initiatives aimed at facilitating internal organisational change (Schwab, 2008).

CSR AND SOCIAL DEVELOPMENT

CSR programmes are a means by which a mining company can be seen as actively giving back to the community. CSR has increasingly been heralded as a pathway to achieving sustainable development; however, whether the private sector can ethically drive development is hotly contested. Proponents suggest that business's role in facilitating social progress is through 'focusing their activities related to their core competencies and unique resources and capabilities . . . utilizing local capabilities and knowledge about markets, production and distribution, and external expertise through partnerships' (Kolk & Van Tulder, 2006, p. 790). Others point to CSR as primarily a business tool that privileges business priorities, as exemplified through the need for a business case for CSR, rather than a development strategy (Newell & Frynas, 2007).

Examining the role of MNCs in driving CSR inevitably raises the question of whether business is an appropriate agent of development and exposes tensions between the two orthodoxies of managerialism and sustainable development (Grant, 2003).

Although CSR was not originally envisioned as a means of eradicating poverty, the dominant view now holds that it is suitable to achieving social goals (Merino & Valor 2011) It can be argued that while firms accept the 'business case' for CSR as a business tool, they are more reluctant to embrace the 'social case' or the responsibilities associated with an understanding of CSR as a development tool. The strategic potential of development-oriented CSR lies in companies' ability to affect global poverty and other large-scale challenges such as climate change and gender empowerment. However, as Barkemeyer (2009) points out, it is doubtful that contemporary CSR initiatives tackle some of the most pressing development challenges. His study of the 416 descriptive case studies published by members of the UN Global Compact revealed that only certain topics are commonly addressed by business initiatives, and issues such as anticorruption and labour rights are underrepresented.

The ambiguity surrounding definitions of CSR reflects fundamental debates about the appropriate role of business in society, further exacerbated by the lack of consensus in development circles about 'how to measure and define, let alone tackle, poverty' (Newell & Frynas, 2007, p. 673). Therefore, it is not surprising that MNCs do not universally conceptualise their CSR programmes as contributing to poverty alleviation. The key contribution of the private sector as the engine of development has been attributed to its wealth-generation activities. Based on a neoclassical economic approach, economic growth will alleviate inequalities through the generation of plenty. However, contributions to poverty alleviation, which rest solely on the potential of business to promote growth or provide jobs, are therefore limited in addressing underlying causes of poverty that exclude people from labour markets in the first place.

A common criticism of CSR is that it does not challenge the structural issues that cause global inequalities and poverty, because business is the key conduit of the economic system that gives rise to these challenges in the first place (Merino & Valor, 2011).

The CSR literature has shifted from studies of the destructive role of business to research on the potential of business to meet global development challenges. An emphasis on why and how to engage in CSR has prompted a proliferation in literature around frameworks, indicators, policies and codes of conduct. Research on the 'what' of CSR has focused on a handful of good-practise case studies, with very little empirical evidence that establishes a causal relationship between on-the-ground effects in communities and CSR initiatives within companies (Frynas, 2008). Furthermore, this case-study approach has generally focused on 'the micro perspective, instead of offering a macro-level approach which provides a balanced assessment of the impact of the private sector on poverty alleviation' (Merino & Valor 2011, p. 161).

CSR has tended to deal with a handful of common social issues while marginalising other challenges (Utting, 2007). Developmental concerns of poorer countries are often left unaddressed, including issues such as 'the cost and impact' of CSR initiatives and instruments on smaller enterprises. The situation of informal sector workers and whether transnational corporations, or large retailers cut and run when their suppliers come under the CSR spotlight (Utting, 2007, p. 701). Although CSR in developing countries is increasingly gaining attention, issues of particular concern to activists in the developed countries, such as child labour, environmental degradation and sweat shops, are those that dominate the CSR agenda. This is partly because an MNC's primary stakeholders are located in the north, and CSR initiatives in LDCs are targeted at these audiences rather than oriented toward their beneficiaries in the south (Barkemeyer, 2009). The main argument is that perhaps international business institutions such as mining MNCs may not understand or be interested in the social issues of host countries.

A notable omission in the CSR debate is the role of business in contributing to global poverty. Words such as 'poverty' or 'development' are used in CSR discourse, but they remain undefined. There is a tendency to view poverty as an individual and a local problem, and marginality as a residual effect that businesses can attempt to mitigate (Merino & Valor, 2011, p. 164). Earlier, a few organisations focused on economic, philanthropic and legal responsibilities. Nowadays, with the changing market situation, this focus is shifting to include three other factors: environmental, educational and health responsibilities (Carino, 2002; Sharma & Kiran, 2013).

An overall reluctance to engage with the roots of poverty and the role of business in perpetuating these structural issues has caused CSR to manifest as programmatic, micro-level initiatives targeted at very specific and selective social goals, thereby limiting the attainment of broader sustainable-development outcomes.

Since this book deals directly with cases in Thailand and Laos, some lessons from both countries should be discussed at this stage. When it comes to CSR among mining companies in Thailand, CSR Asia argues that 'it appears to be in its developing stages, with scarce data available to draw definitive conclusions' (Mavro, 2010). As a hub for foreign direct investment in the region, Thailand attracts a number of mining MNCs and consequently exhibits higher penetration by CSR activities (Chapple & Moon, 2005). However, the impacts of various CSR activities by mining MNCs have not been fully discussed in the public domain.

In a comparative study on CSR website reporting in seven Asian countries, of the top 500 companies in Thailand in 2014, 42% reported on their CSR activities, with 24% of those reporting minimally, 62% providing medium coverage and 14% extensively outlining their efforts. Community involvement was the favoured issue for discussion, mentioned by 71% of Thai companies, while 19% reported on production processes and 10% on employee relations.

There is a general reluctance to expand conceptualisations of CSR beyond philanthropy and community service to incorporate innovation and sustainable practises (Mavro, 2010). However, a number of concrete examples provide insight into how social responsibility is being appropriated by Thai companies to achieve more sustainable outcomes. Working toward social issues such as poverty alleviation or inequity remains an oblique and implicit goal, rather than an overt aim of these initiatives. It is far more likely that building a business case for CSR that reduces cost and delivers greater efficiency is the narrative around pursuing corporate sustainability.

In conclusion, the development of CSR in extractive industries can ignite the ongoing debate over who should benefit from this industry. A common thread within this emerging field of organisational research in mining is the blurred 'boundary' between what can be described as internally- and externally-orientated functions. This distinction is less clear when the question of CSR practise is brought into frame.

REFERENCES

Barkemeyer, R. (2009). Beyond compliance—below expectations? CSR in the context of international development. *Business Ethics (Oxford, England)*, *18*(3), 273–289. doi:10.1111/j.1467-8608.2009.01563.x

Bose, R. (2004). Knowledge management metrics. *Industrial Management & Data Systems*, *106*(1), 457–468. doi:10.1108/02635570410543771

Campbell, B. (2012). Corporate social responsibility and development in Africa: Redefining the roles and responsibilities of public and private actors in the mining sector. *Resources Policy*, *37*(2), 138–143. doi:10.1016/j. resourpol.2011.05.002

Capaldi, N. (2005). Corporate social responsibility and the bottom line. *International Journal of Social Economics*, *32*(5), 408–423. doi:10.1108/03068290510591263

Carino, J. K. (2002). Women and mining in the Cordillera and International Women and Mining Network. In I. MacDonald & C. Rowland (Eds.), *Tunnel vision: Women, mining and communities* (pp. 16–19). Fitzroy: Oxfam Community Aid Abroad.

Caroll, A. (1979). A three-dimensional conceptual model of corporate performance. *Academy of Management Review*, *4*(4), 497–505. doi:10.5465/amr.1979.4498296

Chapple, W., & Moon, J. (2005). Corporate social responsibility (CSR) in Asia: A seven country study of CSR website reporting. *Business & Society*, *44*(4), 415–441. doi:10.1177/0007650305281658

De Soto, H. (2002). *The mystery of capital*. New York: Basic Books.

Deegan, C. (2002). Introduction—the legitimising effect of social and environmental disclosures—a theoretical foundation. *Accounting, Auditing & Accountability Journal*, *15*(3), 282–311. doi:10.1108/09513570210435852

Department of Foreign Affairs and Trade (DFAT). (2014). *Mid-term review of international mining for development centre*. Retrieved from: https://dfat.gov.au/about-us/publications/Pages/mid-term-review-of-international-mining-for-development-centre-im4dc.aspx

Donaldson, T., & Preston, L. E. (1995). The stakeholder theory of the corporation: Concepts, evidence and implications. *Academy of Management Review*, *20*(1), 65–91. doi:10.5465/amr.1995.9503271992

Dutta, M. J. (2008). *Communicating health: A culture-centreed approach*. London: Polity Press.

Eisendhart, K. M. (1998). Building Theories from Case Study Research. *Academy of Management Review*, *14*(4), 532–550. doi:10.5465/amr.1989.4308385

Elkington, J. (1998). *Cannibals with forks: The triple bottom line of 21. Stoney Creek*. New Society Publishers.

Friedman, M. (1970, September 13) The social responsibility of business Is to increase its profits. *New York Times Magazine*, 122-126.

Ganesh, S. (2007). Sustainable development discourse and the global economy: Promoting responsibility, containing change. In S. May, G. Cheney, & J. Roper (Eds.), *The debate over corporate social responsibility* (pp. 379–390). New York: Oxford University Press.

Global Compact, U. N. (2013). *Responsible business advancing peace: examples from companies,investors & Global Compact local networks*. Retrieved from: http://www.unglobalcompact.org/docs/issues_doc/Peace_ and_Business/B4P_ResourcePackage.pdf

Grant, R. M. (2003). Strategic planning in a turbulent environment: Evidence from oil majors. *Strategic Management Journal, 24*(2), 491–517. doi:10.1002mj.314

Kemp, D., & Owen, J. (2013). Community relations and mining: Core to business but not 'core business'. *Resources Policy, 38*(4), 523–531. doi:10.1016/j.resourpol.2013.08.003

Kolk, A., & Van Tulder, R. (2006). Poverty alleviation as business strategy? Evaluating commitments of frontrunner multinational corporations. *World Development, 34*(5), 789–801. doi:10.1016/j.worlddev.2005.10.005

La Shrestha, O. (2010). Lao People's Democratic Republic in 2009: Economic performance, prospects, and challenges. *Southeast Asian Affairs, 2010*(1), 145–152. doi:10.1355/SEAA10I

Lahiri-Dutt, K. (2011). Digging women: Towards a new agenda for feminist critiques of mining. *Gender, Place and Culture, 19*(2), 193–212. doi:10.10 80/0966369X.2011.572433

Lauwo, S. (2018). Challenging masculinity in CSR disclosures: Silencing of women's voices in Tanzania's mining industry. *Journal of Business Ethics, 149*(3), 689–706. doi:10.100710551-016-3047-4

Lynch, M. (2002). *Mining in world history*. London: Reaktion Books.

Majer, M. (2013). The Practice of Mining Companies in Building Relationships with Local Communities in the Context of CSR Formula. *Journal of Sustainable Mining, 12*(3), 38–47. doi:10.7424/jsm130305

Mavro, A. P. (2010). CSR in Thailand. In W. Visser & N. Tolhurst (Eds.), *The world guide to csr: A country-by-country analysis of corporate sustainability and responsibility* (pp. 28–44). Sheffield, UK: Greenleaf Publishing. doi:10.9774/GLEAF.978-1-907643-09-5_59

McMillan, J. (2007). Why corporate responsibility? Why now? How? In S. May, G. Cheney, & J. Roper (Eds.), *The debate over corporate social responsibility* (pp. 37–52). Oxford, UK: Oxford University Press.

Mercier, L., & Gier, J. (2007). Reconsidering women and gender in mining. *History Compass*, 5(3), 995–1001. doi:10.1111/j.1478-0542.2007.00398.x

Merino, A., & Valor, C. (2011). The potential of corporate social responsibility to eradicate poverty: An ongoing debate. *Development in Practice*, 21(2), 35–56. doi:10.1080/09614524.2011.546005

Moon, S. (2008). Corporate environmental behaviours in voluntary programmemes: Does timing matter? *Social Science Quarterly*, 89(5), 1102–1120. doi:10.1111/j.1540-6237.2008.00575.x

Moretti, D. (2006). The gender of the gold: An ethnographic and historical account of women's involvement in artisanal and small-scale mining in Mount Kaindi, Papua New Guinea. *Oceania*, 76(2), 133–149. doi:10.1002/j.1834-4461.2006.tb03041.x

Newell, P., & Frynas, J. G. (2007). Beyond CSR? business, poverty and social justice: An introduction. *Third World Quarterly*, 28(4), 669–681. doi:10.1080/01436590701336507

Oxfam. (2009). *Women, communities and mining: The gender impacts of mining and the role of gender impact assessment*. Retrieved from: https://www.oxfam.org.au/wp-content/uploads/2017/04/2017-PA-001-Gender-impact-assessments-in-mining-report_FA_WEB.pdf

Oxfam. (2017). *Position paper on gender justice and the extractive industries*. Retrieved from: https://www.oxfam.org.au/wp-content/uploads/2017/04/EI_and_GJ_position_paper_v.15_FINAL_03202017_green_Kenny.pdf

Pattenden, C. (1998). *Women in mining: A report to the 'Women in Mining' Taskforce of the AusIMM*. Melbourne: AusIMM.

Samy, M., Odemilin, G., & Bampton, R. (2010). Corporate social reponsibility: A strategy for sustainable business success: An analysis of 20 selected British companies. *Corporate Governance, 10*(2), 203–217. doi:10.1108/14720701011035710

Schwab, K. (2008). Global corporate citizenship: Working with governments and civil society. *Foreign Affairs, 87*(1), 107–118.

Sharma, A., & Kiran, R. (2013). Corporate social responsibility: Driving forces and challenges. *International Journal of Business Research and Development, 2*(1), 18–27. doi:10.24102/ijbrd.v2i1.182

Suchman, M. (1995). Managing legitimacy: Strategic approaches and institutional approaches. *Academy of Management Review, 20*(3), 571–610. doi:10.5465/amr.1995.9508080331

Utting, P. (2007). CSR and equality. *Third World Quarterly, 28*(4), 697–712. doi:10.1080/01436590701336572

Visser, W. (2010). The age of responsibility: CSR 2.0 and the new DNA of business. *Journal of Business Systems. Governance and Ethics, 5*(3), 7–22.

Waddock, S. (2005). Hollow men and women at the helm . . . hollow accounting ethics? *Issues in Accounting Education, 20*(2), 145–150. doi:10.2308/iace.2005.20.2.145

Werbach, A. (2009). *Strategy for sustainability: A business manifesto.* Harvard Business Press.

Werthmann, K. (2009). Working in a boom-town: Female perspectives on gold-mining in Burkina Faso. *Resources Policy, 34*(1-2), 18–29. doi:10.1016/j.resourpol.2008.09.002

Workplace Gender Equality Agency. (2013). *Annual report 2012-2013.* Retrieved from: https://www.wgea.gov.au/sites/default/files/wgea_annual_report_12_13.pdf

Yakovleva, N., & Vazquez-Brust, D. (2012). Stakeholder perspectives on CSR of mining MNCs in Argentina. *Journal of Business Ethics, 106*(2), 191–211. doi:10.100710551-011-0989-4

Chapter 2
The Gendered Dimensions of Mining

ABSTRACT

The costs and benefits of large mines to local communities and the relationship between mining multinational corporations (MNCs), government, and communities are subjects that have become important in developing and developed countries alike. To date, there has been a dearth of comprehensive study on roles and responsibilities of mining MNCs with respect to women and gender equality. Given that the relationship between mining MNCs and communities is changing rapidly—albeit unevenly and unsystematically—the need to develop understanding to better assess the gender impact of different approaches on this relationship and on the ability to maximise sustainable benefits from mining has become paramount. This chapter identifies the linkages between, on the one hand, work and labour-relations issues (e.g., long hours), reform of gender diversity policies and initiatives in mining, as well as the cultural lag between policy and practise; and, on the other hand, the impact of mining on women in mining towns/communities, a gendered impact assessment tool, and the relationship between mining and socioeconomic wellbeing.

DOI: 10.4018/978-1-5225-3811-0.ch002

INTRODUCTION

Women experience direct and indirect consequences of mining operations in different and more pronounced ways than men. Gender inequality drives poverty and denies women their fundamental rights. (Oxfam Australia, 2009)

Various factors can explain the complex relationship between the mining industry and the local community in the host country. Power inequity, ownership of natural resources, political and business relationships, labour welfare, and environmental problems seem to constitute the common lens for most people. In fact, gender inequality has become a popular topic among scholars in social studies. In recent years, various stakeholders associated with the mining industry have conveyed concerns about issues surrounding women and mining, despite a greater sensitivity to gender equity and sustainability issues. A pioneering article in the *Impact Assessment and Project Appraisal* journal in 2010 identifies this tension in regard to women and mining development:

Although companies governing resource extraction are sensitive and responsive to sustainable resource management, certain policies and programmes during the operation of mines, and processes within communities, may lead to unintended consequences at the micro level that promote and sustain gender inequality within the domains of family and community, negatively effecting the wellbeing of women (Sharma & Kiran, 2012).

The history of mining is related to the military (Mercier & Gier, 2007) and that could explain the relationship among gender constructions of work in mining, family and militancy, and masculinity of the mining industry. Women's engagement in mining is eclectic and beyond working in the field. The review and survey of existing literature takes its point of departure from this contemporary contention outlined by Sharma and Kiran (2012). The literature on women's engagement in mining, particularly barriers and factors that shape women's engagement, and the impact of mining on women, highlight the complex and multifaceted nature of the topic. The relationship of women to mining can be understood as interdisciplinary. It is examined at the intersections of the sociology of health and well-being; the sociology of work and labour studies; gender studies; gender research in geography and anthropology; rural studies; and international business, corporate social responsibility and sustainability. Notwithstanding the historically gendered foundations and features of the mining industry, the focus on women and mining today is timely. The literature frequently identifies diverse factors shaping impact and lived experience from multiple perspectives, opening up enquiry into macro and micro socioeconomic dimensions of mining. As mentioned by Ballard and Banks (2003), the 'enduring opacity of mining corporations is their notorious reluctance to expose themselves directly to ethnographic scrutiny' (p. 290).

A growing literature shows that large-scale capitalised mining introduces a rapidity of social change that affects women more negatively than it does men (Oxfam, 2017). The gendered impacts often cut across class and race, but poorer women (and men) are more negatively affected because of their disadvantaged position. However, there is a much smaller—though growing—body of research addressing the specific impact of mining on women, the gender that is also the focus of this review.

This chapter identifies the linkages between, on the one hand, work and labour relations issues such as long hours, reform of gender diversity policies and initiatives in mining, the cultural lag between policy and practise; and, on the other hand, the impact of mining on women in mining towns/communities, a gendered impact assessment tool, and the relationship between mining and socioeconomic well-being.

Two key issues provided an initial analytical framework to underpin the exploration of the topic: women and equitable employment in mining (issue 1), and the impact of mining communities and development on women (issue 2).

The large majority of literature used in preparing this chapter was specific to the Australian context, followed by some aspects of mining from Asia, Europe, the UK and Canada. The bibliographies of articles identified further papers, such as sociological peer-reviewed conference papers and book reviews. Theoretical material related to notions of unequal power relationships, male power, women and power and dimensions of power were also captured. Information was gleaned from Lukes' work *Power: A Radical View* (1974) and Hochschild's work *Ideology and Emotion Management: A Perspective and Path for Future Research* (1990), as well as connections made to theoretical material by Marx (on power, exploitation), Bourdieu (on rules of the game, social practise) and Foucault (on power).

On this basis, Table 1 identifies the most common findings in relation to the literature on women, mining and mining development. The table identifies the gendered dimensions of mining related to space, place, relations, norms, practises and advantages, as the single most mentioned variable in the literature.

Table 1. Findings of the review of literature about women and mining—'the gendered dimensions' of mining and mining development

No.	Finding	Relevance to Issue 1, 2
1	Women in mining towns and communities are at a substantial social and economic disadvantage to men—drawing on select indicators of gender equity, including their greater vulnerability to mental-health problems.	Issue 1, 2
2	Mining is a spatial context traditionally gendered as masculine and is dominated by men where masculine norms, practises and discourses are the predominant feature.	Issue 1, 2
3	The impacts of mining operations and related activities are not gender neutral.	Issue 1, 2
4	Deep divisions in relation to gender, regional and corporate operations exist.	Issue 1
5	Mining is one of the most highly sex-segregated industries, which has implications for health, well-being and economic sustainability.	Issue 1
6	Despite more attention to women, the gendered impact and social impact of large-scale mining remains a neglected field of enquiry; including a gap in knowledge on single women (divorced, separated and widowed)	Issue 1, 2
7	The consideration of gender is a prerequisite for sustainable decisions and outcomes—community development, research and policy initiatives to enhance women's inclusion in mining need further attention	Issue 1, 2

Three themes—gender segregation and male-dominated norms; perceptions of management; and the impact of mining on the lives of women—emerge as the significant points from the literature.

MINING WORK AND WOMEN

A significant body of research on women and mining work, gender diversity and equity issues in mining operations in Australia and internationally has accumulated since the 1980s, and there is now a well-documented response by the industry and scholars from various fields (Sharm & Kiran, 2013; Pimpa et al, 2015). Women today are no longer overtly denied entrance into mining or 'refused underground tours on the grounds that it would bring bad luck to the mine' (Pattenden, 1998, p. 7). However, a key finding of the review is that mining is undertaken in a spatial context traditionally gendered as masculine and dominated by men, where masculine norms, practises, relations and discourses predominate. Masculine norms sustain structural barriers that marginalise women and negatively impact on household, community and employment relations.

Gender Segregation and Male-Dominated Norms in Mining Workplaces and Communities

It is well-documented that women are underrepresented in relatively high-paying occupations and industries across the world. Employment patterns in the mining industry reflect this finding. The mining industry is dominated by male, full-time employment in Australia and internationally, demonstrating social and gendered inequities that create acute challenges to maintaining social services for regional and remote mining communities. There is now a well-developed literature explaining that historically, women have been involved in mining and mining-related activities in a predominantly informal context (Ostas, 2004) and have incurred negative impacts to their well-being and health (Philips, 2003).

When it comes to modern management in the mining industry, many mining companies in Australia and internationally have policies on equal employment opportunity, recognising the equality that exists between men and women in the workforce. This is because in Australia and internationally, the mining industry has a history of gender segregation. In Australia, women are generally associated with working in low-paid industries and occupations, and underrepresented in mining, recognised as relatively high-paying work. In particular, women are underrepresented in management and on-site mining occupations. Similarly, in the UK, mining is recognised as the 'worst sector for gender diversity—with just 5% of board seats held by women in the top 500 mining companies' reported in 2013 (Sharma & Kiran, 2013, p.28).

The weight of evidence from Australia suggests that indirect structural impediments exist, such as assumptions sustaining male-dominated cultural norms in workplaces and communities, which exclude and have negative implications for women despite antidiscrimination legislation and the implementation of gender diversity initiatives (Sharma & Kiran, 2013). While the increase in female participation is of benefit to the economy, in many cases it has led to difficulties in combining the demands of work, family and community life. Balancing and integrating these competing demands primarily falls into the domain of women as a social practise (Bose, 2004).

Table 2 shows that in Australia, the participation rate of female employees in mining is 13.4% full-time, whereas full-time male participation is 83.3 per cent (ABS, 2013). The rate of female participation on a part-time basis is 2%, whereas male part-time employees comprise 1.3%.

Overall, women make up just 15.4% of the mining workforce in Australia. The number of full-time average weekly hours in the mining industry in Australia shows that women and men work similarly long hours, comprising 44.6 hours per week worked by women and 45.8 hours per week worked by men (ABS, 2013).

In Lao PDR, not unlike Australia, recruitment of the mining workforce is a key issue. In particular, the labour force is made up of international and domestic workers.

In the absence of reliable data, the effects of mining draw on survey data from the Household Survey 2007 and data provided by the two main large-scale mining companies, MMG Sepon and PBM Phu Khma copper-gold operation. The number of direct employees in mining in Lao PDR in 2010 was 2,300; indirect employees comprised 1,600; and induced employment was 9,700. Overall, 13,650 employees in 2010 constituted the mining labour force. However, there is no available gender breakdown in employment participation in mining in Lao PDR and Thailand (ICMM, 2011, 28).

Figure 1.

·Mining is undertaken in a spatial context traditionally gendered as masculine and dominated by men were masculine norms, practises, relations and discourses are predominant.·

·Masculine norms sustain structural barriers that marginalise women and negatively impact on household, community and employment relations·.

Table 2. Mining industry, Australia by employment and gender, July 2013

	WOMEN		MEN	
	F-T	P-T	F-T	P-T
Participation rate	13.4%	2%	83.3%	1.3%
Average weekly hours	44.6 hrs	23.5 hrs	45.8 hrs	18.7 hrs

Source: Australian Bureau of Statistics (2013)

25

By their very nature, male-dominated occupations and industries are resistant to policies designed to increase female participation or equal organisational rank (Pimpa et al, 2015), and mining is no exception. A key challenge is to attract women to work in mining and to return after having children, which requires flexible work arrangements and access to quality childcare in remote areas.

Sanjay (2009) explores the interacton among a number of environmental, occupational, social-cultural and psychological factors that could influence the well-being of the families living in the remote mining towns. Interviews were completed with 45 women and 50 men—individuals identified as key community personnel, mine workers and their partners, and hour-long focus groups involving women from various community organisations. Interviews included questions on adjustments and strategies for attempting to overcome the negative aspects of work-leisure conflict, so as to build up a general picture of women's lives in the town in order to contextualise the more detailed individual accounts of how women experienced the 12-hour shifts.

Both groups of women spoke at length about the problems of bringing up children and coordinating family life around the shifts. For the more recent arrivals, distance from familiar support networks and difficulties in making friends and finding suitable employment in a small remote town were common. Such experiences were likely to add to women's expectations of companionship from their partners; expectations which, as the following section outlines, were at odds with the patriarchal culture of [the town].

Lauwo (2018) also criticised the transparency and disclosure of the mining industry. Although mining companies have disclosed some information on gender issues in recent years, the information disclosed has remained somewhat selective and at the discretion of management. This selectivity in information disclosure in CSR reports is consistent with earlier studies that have found disclosure to be dependent on management discretion, with support for social responsibility initiatives provided purely for business reasons, rather than out of any altruistic desire to improve conditions in the workplace or in local communities (Lauwo, 2018)

NORMATIVE STANDARDS AND POLICIES FOR GENDER EQUITY IN MINING

Accommodating change and diversity has been a key challenge for the mining industry. Despite the movement of women into mining, 'an underlying conservatism in employment practise exists which has seen the promotion of individuals who most closely resemble the existing management hierarchy in terms of gender education and well-being (Sanjay, 2009).

The challenge is to find imaginative ways to chip away at the gendered assumptions underpinning existing practises, policies, culture and norms that lead to barriers and resistance to women in mining and in relation to mining operations, as well as poor outcomes for employees, employers and local communities. It is critical, therefore, to rethink the design and organisation of work not only for the employee working experience, but also for gender equity, the mining workplace and organisational effectiveness.

The rate of turnover in the mining industry is high, particularly during times of heightened production. Excessive turnover has adverse effects on costs, staff morale and work safety, as well as on production. In Australia, mining is one of the most highly paid, yet gender-skewed occupations.

Perceptions of Management

Mining continues to be perceived as a male-oriented industry. The attitudes of management are crucial to overcoming the barriers to equitable employment for women in mining, and for the development of education and poverty-relieving initiatives in communities. The formation of associations and networks such as the Women in Mining Network (WIMnet) in Australia, the Lao PDR Women's Union (LWU) and the National Commission for the Advancement of Women (NCAW) in Lao PDR, have been established for the protection of women's rights and interests. In particular, the LWU protects the rights and interests also of Lao multi-ethnic women and children, including the implementation of the policy on gender equality, and the advancement of women in the implementation of national socioeconomic development.

From the perspective of mining companies, the recruitment and retention of women are key issues to address because both concern labour-shortage needs and productivity, particularly at a time when the structure of the economy, the market and family households are changing. In Australia, for example, the notion of a 'two-speed economy' has attracted much debate in recent years, describing the contemporary context where jobs are being shed across industries, yet cushioned by a mining rush. In her paper on Women in Mining to the AusIMM Youth Congress in 2001, Wynn (2001) noted the importance of exploring and paying attention to the attitudes of management:

The attitudes of management can be crucial to the success of a female employee, and overcoming the influence of more senior staff members can be difficult. Attitudes and opinions can be passed from management to other members of the workforce. Opportunities for promotion can often be hindered without justification. P.33)

Employment relations, perceptions of management, industry culture and international governance have been noted in the literature as key impacts on women's experiences. The nature of the mining work includes long working hours, issues surrounding rosters and shifts and fly-in-fly-out work arrangements. Further questions about management perceptions and utilisation of programmes and policies to assist women include:

- Access to quality child care in remote sites was a problem for families and female workers;
- Barriers around child care—access and expenses are not tax deductible except by way of salary sacrifice; only available to employers who run their own child care centre on their own premises;
- Child Care Rebate and Benefit are capped at low levels and not strongly linked to workforce participation;
- Employment participation of women in the mining industry is a sector of specific interest because it is Australia's best-paid industry with average earnings significantly higher than in other industries, and industry representatives have publicly discussed the need to recruit and retain women employees to enable them to address labour and skills shortages within the industry;
- Labour shortages have been cited as a potential reason that projects or parts of projects are being relocated offshore; labour shortages have been cited as having detrimental effects on industry productivity; and
- Employee needs for time to balance work/life commitments may be seen as opposed to organisational needs for flexibility and productivity to meet global and industry competitive pressures.

The Impact of Mining on the Lives of Women

The literature identifies diverse factors that impact the lives of women in mining towns and communities, from harsh climatic and structural conditions of the towns to limited resources and opportunities, physical separation from relatives and friends, having to accommodate their lives to male miners, the cultural ethos prevalent in male-dominated organisations, implications for psychological stressors and relationship breakdown.

Sanjay (2009) reported in his study that the nature of shift work in mining industry can influence women in various ways. Shift work can influence their physiological functioning. The immediate disturbances to shift workers are symptoms such as sleep disorders, fatigue, jetlag or gastro-intestinal malfunctions31 that induces irritability, grumpiness, lethargy and relative non-participation in family activities (Sanjay, 2009). This disrupts the family and the social relations of a shift worker as there is a 'spillover' of job generated worker's negative moods and energy levels to the family domain. These work-family conflicts affect a worker's physical and mental health, quality of family life, life satisfaction, and marital satisfaction (Sanjay, 2009)

When it comes to career path for women in this sector, there is a strong business case for companies to prioritise and support women's participation in consultation and decision-making forums. Companies that ignore issues of gender justice and fail to address women's interests may not meet their human rights obligations, could face possible legal action or conflict with local communities and might be wasting community-development funds on projects with few positive and lasting impacts (Oxfam, 2017). These points can potentially be related to their relationship with family and other networks.

The issue of community engagement and community development includes (1) integration with business planning and management-led initiatives (Kemp & Owen, 2013); (2) the role of tools such as a gender impact assessment; and (3) a social impact assessment (Oxfam, 2009). Mining and CSR literature continues to focus on 'corporate performance', reflecting the perceived importance of global benchmarking and the industry's seemingly natural proclivity toward messaging through corporate-level sustainability reports (Kemp & Owen, 2013).

Further, impact issues and questions in the literature include:

- Managing changing family or community structures;
- Increased sex work or the spread of HIV/AIDS; and

- The role of women in the mining industry—while having the skill and ability to work effectively, there is also a commitment to the lifestyle.

The Provision of Health for Women

The mining industry has the potential to bring great benefits to a community, as well as great harm. Women often bear the greatest burdens associated with the mining industry, such as family and/or social disruption, health effects, and environmental degradation. Yet, the rewards of mining, such as compensation and employment, often favour men.

Most academic research focuses on the occupational health and safety of the male, white, mining workforce and less on the health of their families or communities living in the vicinity of mines. This has resulted in women's and communities' health being overlooked.

Much research (Sanjay, 2009; Ballard & Banks, 2003; Horowitz, 2002) describes self-reports of the health impact of the pollution caused by local mines. Local fishermen in Rapu Rapu in the Philippines have been affected by toxic spills, their livelihoods and health negatively impacted due to a lack of fresh fish. Similarly, local communities reported dysentery and bloated stomachs from water contaminated with mine waste in Fiji. Communities living downstream from the Tolukuma Gold Mine (TGM) in Papua New Guinea (PNG) describe instances of unexplained deaths, swollen stomachs, open sores and yellow feet from drinking and walking in the river. Evidence of river pollution has been substantiated by independent and internal studies that found high levels of mercury in fish species and the water.

Water pollution from a copper mine is causing health problems in Marinduque Island in the Philippines. Heavy-metal poisoning and arsenic contamination from the mine are said to be responsible for stomach upsets, dementia, cancer and the deaths of several children. It has also affected the health of fish that locals rely on for nutrition and the livelihoods of fishermen. Other reported health issues include inflamed joints, respiratory illnesses, nausea and vomiting. Independent research by Oxfam and the Institute for Environmental Conservation and Research at Ateneo de Naga City University conducted tests that found hazardous levels for human health of cadmium, copper, lead, manganese, nickel and sulphate, and hazardous levels for aquatic life of cadmium, copper, iron, zinc and sulphate .

Gold-mine workers in Fiji have complained of skin and eye itchiness, respiratory and sinus problems and deafness. Many assert that Emperor, the mining company, did not take their health concerns seriously and paid no sickness benefits. Despite injuries sustained whilst working, such as back injuries, damaged or lost eyes, fingers and hands, Emperor would attempt to avoid paying compensation and miners were pressured to work whilst unfit.

Conversely, some communities have praised the mine for bringing much needed infrastructure such as roads, health clinics and improvements to schools, but expressed concern that the mine was taking responsibility for services that should be the government's domain.

Mining and Women's Health

The discourse on mining and women's health is overwhelmingly focused on the negative impacts of mining on the health of women and describes similar health manifestations despite geographic and industry variance. Alarmingly, one of the most commonly described health impacts of the mining industry on women is physical and sexual violence. This is often precipitated by alcohol abuse, illicit drug use and a predominant and transient male workforce. High rates of human immunodeficiency virus (HIV) and sexually transmitted infections (STIs) are also common in women living and working in mining communities and are related to sexual violence and the predominantly male workforce creating a demand for sex work.

It was reported by D'Souza et al (2013) that Indian women who work in the mining industry reported issues such as early marriage, increased fertility, less birth intervals, son preference and lack of decision-making regarding reproductive health choices. Moreover, domestic violence, gender preference, husbands drinking behaviors, and low spousal communication were common experiences considered by female miners as factors leading to poor quality of marital relationship.

The degradation of the environment from mining can disproportionately affect women's health. Women are often responsible for gathering water, preparing meals, washing dishes and clothes and bathing their children, making them more exposed to toxic and polluted water for longer periods of time. Water-borne disease can include gastrointestinal infections, colic and heavy-metal positioning from silica and lead. Loss of water resources due to pollution has affected important food sources such as fish stocks, affecting women and their families' nutritional status. Exploitation of natural resources can result in the loss of plants used for traditional medicines.

Other common symptoms reported by women include respiratory illnesses, skin conditions, silicosis, tuberculosis, asbestosis and reoccurring headaches. Women living in the vicinity of a Manganese mine in Mexico described ways in which the mine has damaged their health including headaches, flu and lung pain, coughs, sore throats, burning eyes and diarrhoea. They claimed that exposure to manganese makes them more prone to illness and exacerbates and complicates existing illnesses. They also expressed concern for the health of their children, whom they felt were the most vulnerable to the effects of manganese, given that they played outdoors often. They deemed manganese responsible for memory loss, learning difficulties, laziness, despondency and lack of concentration in their children. Women in Bihar, India, living near coal and uranium mines, experienced malaria, typhoid and hepatitis after mining activities began. Women living in mining communities in Orissa, India, reported skin, respiratory and gastrointestinal diseases among children and family members, and attributed them to air, soil and water pollution caused by the mine.

Mining, Stress, Mental Health and Well-Being.

The mining industry can also contribute to mental-health issues and stress through forced relocation due to mining activities and entrenched poverty.

Mining sites are often situated in remote areas far from town centres, making it difficult to access basic social and health-care services if not provided by the mine. Women most commonly provide care to other family members when they are ill, which increases their domestic workloads at the expense of their own health. Female partners of male mine workers and other women living in isolated mining communities suffer disproportionate mental and psychological health impacts.

MINING AND WOMEN'S HEALTH IN LAOS AND THAILAND

Large-scale mining is a recent phenomenon in Laos. There are currently two such mines in Lao PDR that account for over 90% of total mining production: the Phu Bia Mining (PBM) Phu Kham copper-gold operation (120 kilometres north of the capital Vientiane) and the MMG Sepon gold and copper mine (near Sepon, east of Savannakhet in the south).

Thailand has a long history of mining and is the world's leading producer of cement, feldspar, gypsum, and tin. Thailand has one significant gold mine in Chatree, which started operations in 2002. The mine is owned and operated by Kingsgate Consolidated, a partly Australian-owned enterprise. It has purported potential for further gold and base-metal discoveries in the future.

There is a distinct lack of published material on the impact of mining on the health of women in Laos and Thailand. From both the industrial and academic sides, the literature that does examine the health consequences of mining in Laos and Thailand has little focus on women's health.

A study by Jackson (2011) found predominantly positive impacts by the Lao MMG Sepon mine. The mine owners had built existing infrastructure including airfields, highways, schools and health clinics, and provided food and clean water.

Pattenden (1998) found that, in Lao PDR, unmarried women were reported to have benefited more from the mine's presence than married women, although married women with children had reportedly benefited from greater access to maternal and child health care. During the course of the study, concerns arose that large government revenue from mining taxes was not spent on capital investments such as health infrastructure, but was used to buy consumables such as government vehicles.

Tongah Harbour Plc, a Thai company with Australian origins, operates a gold mine in the Wangsaphung district of Loei province of northeastern Thailand. In September 2006, Tungkam Limited (TKL), a subsidiary of Tongah Harbour, began its oprerations at the first open-pit gold mine, in countryside once designated by the Thai government as a conservation area.

A report by (Hodgson, 1975) details some of the health effects suffered by the population living in the mine's vicinity. These include skin irritations and respiratory illnesses from dust blowing through residential areas near the mine. Male mine workers have experienced skin diseases, severe eye and lung problems, insomnia and neurological degeneration. Women experienced breathing difficulties, eye pain and skin rashes after washing clothes worn in the mines. Blood tests have confirmed elevated levels of cyanide and other heavy-metallic contaminants in children. A Thai government report released in February 2009 warned residents to avoid drinking or cooking with locally sourced water due to elevated levels of cyanide, arsenic, cadmium and manganese.

Mining impacts women in all aspects of life and in all stages of the lifecycle. They are the key to reversing not only the disadvantage they face but also that faced by their communities. Hiring women has been shown to have a greater welfare impact on families than hiring men. In addition, women spend income differently than men. Compared to men, women who control the family income, child health and wellbeing have been shown to increase them. Therefore, investing in the health and wellbeing of women and increasing opportunities for women in the workforce make economic sense and a sound basis for human-rights policy. When more women work, economies grow. A study by ILO (1995) that included 15 major developing countries demonstrated that if paid-employment rates for women were raised to the same level as men's, per capita income would rise by 14% by 2020 and 20% by 2030. The elimination of all forms of discrimination against women could increase productivity per worker by up to 40% (ILO, 1995).

Many of the existing health issues women face from the mining sector are a symptom of the stigma and discrimination that women face, and reflect their low status in society. This is particularly pertinent with regard to the prevalence of violence, including sexual violence, inflicted on women who live and/or work in mining communities. The key to improvements in the health and well-being of women requires elevating women's status in all social and economic sectors.

Influencing the health of women requires due consideration given to addressing the social and economic determinants of health, and an appreciation that influencing health outcomes lies outside the health ministry. This will necessitate working to addresses women's disadvantages in terms of access to education, equal employment opportunities, legal status, decent housing and the benefits of development (Sanjay, 2009). There also must be attention given to the health of the environment that supports life in communities, as women are more susceptible to the effects of pollution on rivers and agriculture (Wynn, 2001).

A constant drive to achieve gender equity must underpin the work of all stakeholders in the mining sector, including mining companies, government, NGOs and local communities. This means working with men and women to overcome disadvantage and injustice, and granting women equal representation in decision-making processes.

SUMMARY: THE KEY POINTS FROM INDUSTRY LITERATURE

Point 1: Unearthing New Resources: attracting and retaining women in the Australian minerals industry. It is known that the effective participation of women in the minerals industry is limited by a number of key structural issues, including:

- The low level of part-time work in the minerals industry compared to other sectors, including other traditionally male-oriented industries, is an obvious impediment, in that 40% of female employment nationally is part time;
- The industry's culture of overwork, long hours and intensity has had a more negative impact on women than on men because of their additional caring responsibilities. The remote nature of the industry is also a factor inhibiting female participation in the industry, though this is much less so with regard to the engagement of indigenous women.

Significant cultural impediments to women's participation that are linked to the structural issues manifest as a lack of mentor relationships and support networks, and the gender-segregated nature of decision-making and task allocation, disadvantage, discrimination or harassment.

There is recognisable impact by existing workplace policies, structures and cultures on women's employment in the mining industry, and an identification of alternative strategies, including policies and practises, is required to address these issues.

A number of factors are recommended for the minerals industry to consider in relation to enhancing the participation of women:

Better demonstrate to women the range of jobs available in the industry and link these to nontraditional disciplines (e.g., environmental science, social science, occupational health and safety);

- Establish a comprehensive university-based programme to promote vacation opportunities in the industry along with a cooperative arrangement for extended work experience;
- Provide a more gender-inclusive work environment, which could be achieved by increasing the participation of women in professional and

operational roles, and by providing structured mentoring programmes for women or better gender-awareness training for male employees;

- Address key structural issues such as working arrangements and workplace facilities, and cultural issues such as workplace policies and practises; provide more family-friendly work arrangements, including greater provision of part-time work and career opportunities that enable people to transition in and out of employment in the industry;
- Provide enhanced social infrastructure in rural and remote mining communities and implement a range of cross-cultural measures to increase the attraction and retention of indigenous women.

It is recommended that the minerals industry demonstrate stronger leadership regarding women's participation in the minerals industry:

- Gender considerations should become a mainstream focus in the industry;
- Consideration could be given to hosting a conference of Human Resources personnel to address the issue of workplace diversity and to showcase best practises;
- Stronger leadership should be demonstrated both vertically (within the supply chain in the industry) and horizontally (across companies within the industry); and
- Within companies, both at corporate and at the site level, senior management should lead by example.

It is recommended that the negative image held by prospective women employees be addressed through a range of innovative marketing and networking initiatives.

Point 2: What are the opportunities and challenges for women in fly-in-fly-out mining in Canada?

Recognise the challenges to hiring women:

- Lack of skilled, qualified and experienced women for the jobs available;
- Mothers of young children need a supportive spouse/extended family to provide childcare when they are at work.

Recognise the challenges to retain women:

- Stress on relationships outside the mine;
- Separation guilt/feeling of helplessness, particularly for mothers;
- Incompatibility with mid/late pregnancy stages and caring for infants;
- Difficulty of establishing a regular lifestyle.

Maximise the advantages of hiring and retaining women:

- Financial rewards, because salaries are perceived to be higher, or because some operations pay camp allowances and abundant overtime;
- Personal expenses are dramatically reduced when on site for extended periods of time;
- Long periods off lead to a more fulfilling family life when at home;
- Stronger sense of community, because since the workforce spends several consecutive days in the camp, more interaction forms stronger bonds;
- Opportunity to pursue other activities and goals (educational, recreational, cultural) during time off;
- Services (e.g., food, housekeeping) provided in the camp are convenient and help focus on work or other activities after work.

Confront and manage disadvantages:

- Long time away affects family and personal life negatively and makes having children problematic;
- Rigid work schedules result in missing important family and community events;
- Nomadic lifestyle poses challenges to social life and to well-being;
- Generally, mine camps often provide very little privacy (rooms and bathrooms are usually shared);
- Some overtime is unpaid.

Point 3: Women's concerns are mostly around family/children and perceived risk of sexual harassment.

Recommendations include the establishment of reliable standards and policies regarding maternity and family issues (including monitoring and periodic evaluation); improvement of flexibility in schedules, rosters and work opportunities available to pregnant women or women just returned from maternity leave; establishment of mentorship programmes and more creative personnel policies that support employees with young families; and orientation programmes for new employees that include a family orientation aspect as well.

In this area, we found that there are key barriers effecting women in mining industry. They include:

- 'Like employs like'—male-dominated culture and homogeneous workforce;
- Lack of mentors and role models;
- Lack of networking opportunities;
- Assertiveness and confidence issues;
- Culture of discrimination and harassment.

Recommendations include:

- Advocating for best work practises;
- Including a database of leading practises;
- Advocating for more family-friendly federal policies;
- Working on reducing the gender pay gap;

Key issues:

- Low valuation of (women's) roles not immediately tied to production benefits;
- Remoteness and Fly-in-Fly-Out;
- Flexible working arrangements;
- No on-ramps for primary caregivers of newborns;
- Role of fathers is devalued by peers;
- Lack of on-site or access to child care;
- Lack of networking and professional development.

Point 4: Women, communities and mining: The gender impacts of mining and the role of gender impact assessment

- A gender impact assessment identifies the likely impacts an extractive industry project will have on women, men, boys and girls, and the relationships between them, in mine-affected communities. Its basis is a gender analysis that explores the relationships between women and men in society, and the inequalities in those relationships, by asking:

Who does what? Who has what? Who decides? How? Who gains? Who loses? and Which men? Which women? (Oxfam, 2009).

- Recognise the potential gender impacts of mining projects and introduce some tools and approaches that can be used to conduct a gender impact assessment of these projects. The tools should be of particular interest to community-relations advisors, as they are designed to help incorporate gender into community assessment and planning tools that include social baseline studies, social impact assessments and risk analysis, community mapping exercises and monitoring and evaluation plans. By undertaking a gender impact assessment, mining companies can ensure that their activities respect the rights of women and men; promote women's empowerment and participation in community decision-making processes; and increase the benefits of mining.

- Identify issues related to mining and resettlement. Resettlement disconnects people from their traditional support networks in the community, including informal conflict-resolution mechanisms. This tends to have disproportionate impacts on women, who may be dealing with a range of other impacts such as increased financial dependence on men and household conflict and violence (Oxfam, 2009).

- Encourage informed and meaningful participation of women and men from mine-affected communities in gender impact assessment processes and support the achievement of gender equality.

GENDER IMPACT ASSESSMENT

A gender impact assessment is a tool with transformational potential. It gives a voice to women's perspectives, needs and interests; ensures that gender is considered in the planning and implementation of mining projects; and enables projects to be more responsive to women's needs and interests. This offers mining companies an opportunity to contribute to the promotion of gender equality and women's empowerment. It will help mining companies fulfil their responsibility to respect human rights.

Mining companies will fulfil their responsibility to respect human rights by paying close attention to the gendered impacts of their operations. This may help companies receive and then retain a 'social licence' to operate. In addition, the potential negative impacts of mining operations and the associated costs to the company in terms of possible legal, financial or reputational risks, as well as to communities, can be minimised (Pimpa, Moore, Gregory, & Tenni, 2015).

The impacts of mining operations are not gender neutral. Women can experience the direct and indirect consequences of mining operations in different, and often more pronounced, ways than men.

As men gain employment in mines, there is a withdrawal of male labour from traditional subsistence activities. This can result in an increased work burden for women who become solely responsible for subsistence activities and providing for families.

Due to the decline of traditional mechanisms of social control and the influx of a transient male workforce, social and health problems can become more prevalent in communities. These problems can include increased alcohol use, domestic violence, sexual violence, sexually transmitted infections, HIV and AIDS and prostitution.

Women can experience discrimination in the mine workplace. Employment and training opportunities are often prioritised for men, and women are only allowed to work in the most menial, low-paid positions. Maternity leave may not be provided, and women returning from childbirth or caring for children may struggle to regain employment.

Silences and Gaps

Tackling gender inequality within the extractive industries demands a fundamental shift in how the industry is conceptualised, organised, and governed. It requires a reshaping of the values, culture and norms that produce and maintain gender bias within the sector (Oxfam, 2017). The findings from this review of academic research literature and grey literature (i.e., policy and industry reports) points to gaps and silences, such as the impacts and perspectives of women as spouses and partners of miners, and the importance of looking at domestic lives in the relevant context of mining in contemporary Thailand and Lao PDR—what we know of these issues and their interrelationship with health, choice/agency, work and microfinance is especially lean. Material specific to Lao PDR and Thailand on gender and mining is especially scant.

The absence of gender dynamics and feminist perspectives in CSR debates in the mining industry is evident. Grosser and Moon (2005) argues that despite large numbers of women working and studying in the field of CSR, insights from feminist theory are not well incorporated, and feminist perspectives not extensively articulated in this area. Also, Marshall (2011) examines the gendering of leadership in CSR policies and practises, arguing that women's voices remain absent from CSR disclosures, and that current approaches to CSR tend to individualise what should be systematic in practise, paying little explicit attention to the structural forces that often perpetuate inequality (Marshall, 2017).

Accommodating change and diversity has been a key challenge for the mining industry. Despite the movement of women into mining, 'an underlying conservatism in employment practise exists', which has seen the promotion of individuals who most closely resemble the existing management hierarchy in terms of gender education.

The challenge is to find imaginative ways to chip away at the gendered assumptions underpinning existing practises, policies, culture and norms that lead to barriers and resistance to women in mining, and in relation to mining operations as well as poor outcomes for employees, employers and local communities. It is critical to rethink the design and organisation of work not only for employee working experience, but also for gender equity and the mining workplace, its CSR policies, and organisational effectiveness.

TOWARD A NEW FRAMEWORK

A new framework should recognise impacts and changes in the international mining industry and address equality between men and women to reflect an inclusive and sustainable approach. It aims to propose a series of changes to policy and practise, and programmes to support such an approach. Making a new framework a reality requires commitment from employers, communities, diverse stakeholder groups and individuals. Additional research questions— some key questions developed from this review—include:

- How do women and men in Thailand and Lao PDR think about, perceive and experience mining and mining-related activities?
- What meaning do they attribute to mining over time?
- How does mining take shape and emerge in the context of their lives?
- How much choice or agency do the women feel they have in the way mining companies and mining-related activities impact their lives?
- Do women understand their experiences as constrained or inequitable?

- What, if anything, about their experiences and dynamics in their households in relation to the mining organisations and local communities might explain the relative persistence of gender inequality?
- How do managers of mining organisations perceive gender equality, and what are the dynamics that shape their views and decision-making around sustainable and gender equity practises?
- How do mining and mining companies and management understand and address gender issues?
- What are the needs of women and men in communities where mining operations take place?
- What gender equality efforts currently exist, and where are the gaps to fostering co-operative relationships and sustainable development with local communities?
- Large multinational resource companies play an influential role as agents of economic development and social change, particularly in developing countries; what evidence exists of the negative/positive impacts of mining borne by women?
- Why are development projects more successful when women are involved and what makes these stand out?

REFERENCES

Australian Bureau of Statistics (ABS). (2013). *Census of population and housing*. Canberra: Australian Bureau of Statistics.

Ballard, C., & Banks, G. (2003). Resource wars: The anthropology of mining. *Annual Review of Anthropology*, *32*(1), 287–313. doi:10.1146/annurev.anthro.32.061002.093116

Bose, S. (2004). Positioning women within the environmental justice framework: A case for the mining sector. *Gender, Technology and Development*, *8*(3), 407–412.

D'Souza, M., Karkada, S., Somayaji, G., & Venkatesaperumal, G. (2013). Women's well-being and reproductive health in Indian mining community: Need for empowerment. *Reproductive Health*, *10*(1), 1–24. PMID:23602071

Grosser, K., & Moon, J. (2005). Gender mainstreaming and corporate social responsibility: Reporting workplace issues. *Journal of Business Ethics, 62*(4), 327–340. doi:10.100710551-005-5334-3

Hamann, R. (2004). Corporate social responsibility, partnerships, and institutional change: The case of mining companies in South Africa. *Natural Resources Forum, 28*(4), 278–290. doi:10.1111/j.1477-8947.2004.00101.x

Hodgson, G. (1975). Skin diseases of coal miners in Britain with special reference to the history of changes in mining. *Occupational Medicine, 25*(2), 66–71. doi:10.1093/occmed/25.2.66 PMID:162725

Horowitz, L. (2002). Daily, Immediate Conflicts: An Analysis of Villagers' Arguments about a Multinational Nickel Mining Project in New Caledonia. *Oceania, 73*(1), 35–55. doi:10.1002/j.1834-4461.2002.tb02805.x

ICMM. (2011). *ICMM 2011 annual review: Our journey.* Retrieved from http://www.icmm.com/en-gb/publications/annual-review/2011

International Labor Organization (ILO). (1995). *Women Work More, But are Still Paid Less.* Retrieved from https://www.ilo.org/global/about-the-ilo/newsroom/news/WCMS_008091/lang--en/index.htm

Jackson. (2011). *The Sepon Gold and Copper Mine: Neighbours Past, Present and Future.* Sepon, LAO PDR: LXML.

Kemp, D., & Owen, J. (2013). Community relations and mining: Core to business but not 'core business'. *Resources Policy, 38*(4), 523–531. doi:10.1016/j.resourpol.2013.08.003

Lauwo, S. (2018). Challenging masculinity in CSR disclosures: Silencing of women's voices in Tanzania's mining industry. *Journal of Business Ethics, 149*(3), 689–706. doi:10.100710551-016-3047-4

Marshall, J. (2011). En-gendering Notions of Leadership for Sustainability. *Gender, Work and Organization, 18*(3), 263–281. doi:10.1111/j.1468-0432.2011.00559.x

McPhail, K. (2008). *Sustainable development in the mining and minerals sector: The case for partnership at local, national and global levels.* London: International Council on Mining and Metals. Retrieved from http://www.icmm.com/document/269

Mercier, L., & Gier, J. (2007). Reconsidering women and gender in mining. *History Compass, 5*(3), 995–1001. doi:10.1111/j.1478-0542.2007.00398.x

Ostas, D. (2004). Cooperate, comply, or evade? A corporate executive's social responsibilities with regard to law. *American Business Law Journal, 41*(4), 559–594. doi:10.1111/j.1744-1714.2004.04104004.x

Oxfam. (2009). *Women, communities and mining: The gender impacts of mining and the role of gender impact assessment.* Retrieved from https://www.oxfam.org.au/wp-content/uploads/2017/04/2017-PA-001-Gender-impact-assessments-in-mining-report_FA_WEB.pdf

Oxfam. (2017). *Position paper on gender justice and the extractive industries.* Retrieved from https://www.oxfam.org.au/wp-content/uploads/2017/04/EI_and_GJ_position_paper_v.15_FINAL_03202017_green_Kenny.pdf

Pattenden, C. (1998). *Women in mining: A report to the Women in Mining Taskforce of the AusIMM.* Melbourne: AusIMM.

Phillips, R. A. (2003). Stakeholder legitimacy. *Business Ethics Quarterly, 13*(1), 25–41. doi:10.5840/beq20031312

Pimpa, N., Moore, T., Gregory, S., & Tenni, B. (2015). Corporate social responsibility and mining industry in Thailand. *World Journal of Management, 6*(1), 34–47. doi:10.21102/wjm.2015.03.61.04

Sanjay, S. (2009). *An exploration into the wellbeing of the families living in the 'suburbs in the bush,'* Working paper at Griffith University. Retrieved from: https://research-repository.griffith.edu.au/bitstream/handle/10072/29310/59998_1.pdf?sequence=1&isAllowed=y

Sharma, A., & Kiran, R. (2012). A passion of large organisations or a commitment to the society. *African Journal of Business Management, 6*(22), 6696–6708.

Sharma, A., & Kiran, R. (2013). Corporate social responsibility: Driving forces and challenges. *International Journal of Business Research and Development, 2*(1), 18–27. doi:10.24102/ijbrd.v2i1.182

Wynn, E. J. (2001). *Women in the Mining Industry.* AUSIMM Youth Congress. Retrieved from: https://www.ausimm.com.au/content/docs/wynn.pdf

Chapter 3
Methodology

ABSTRACT

This chapter explains the methodology adopted in this project to learn about experiences from community perspectives, taking an exploratory, interpretive approach to investigate the impacts of the mining industry on women in Thai and Lao mining communities. In order to capture the experiences and interpretations of relevant actors in the mining industry, semi-structured personal and group interviews functioned as an appropriate data-collection technique. This technique helps the researchers to focus on language use by key informants, as well as contextual and relational aspects expressed by the interviewees.

DOI: 10.4018/978-1-5225-3811-0.ch003

RESEARCH LOCATIONS

Vilabouly (ວິລະບູລີ), Lao PDR

Vilabouly is a district in Savannakhet province. It hosts the Sepon mine, the country's first significant foreign mining venture. Sepon is an open-pit copper and gold-mining operation in Southern Laos. Lane Xang Minerals Ltd. (LXML) is the registered name of the company that operates the Sepon mine. Lan Xang is the Lao name for the Kingdom of Laos and means 'one million elephants'. MMG LXML owns 90% of Sepon and the government of Laos owns the other 10%. The Sepon gold project commenced production in 2002; its copper operation commenced in 2005.

The surrounding villages are largely dependent for survival on rice production and foraging of non-timber forest products. Per capita incomes vary widely depending on participation in mining employment, which is influenced by three main factors: access (living in the proximity to the mine); ability to meet minimum educational standards (numeracy and literacy) set by the mine; andpassing a basic health check. However, if the six villages closest to the mine and the district capital are excluded from the calculations, the average per capita income of other neighbouring villages is US$270 per year, 44% of which is derived from mine-related sources.

The villagers continue to identify food security and access to clean water and sanitation as their greatest needs, with 40%-50% of families reporting insufficient food intake (Department of Foreign Affairs and Trade, 2012).

Savannakhet has a total land area of 21,774 km2. About 90% of the area is flat land and about 10% is considered mountainous, located in the eastern part of the province (as shown in Figure 1.) Savannakhet is rich in natural resources including agricultural land, forests, rivers, mineral deposits and biodiversity.

According to statistical data provided by Savannakhet PAFO, the province has a total agricultural land area of about 1.5 million hectares, representing about 68% of the total provincial land area. However, a large share of this agricultural land is considered to have low fertility. Currently, about 209,589 ha, representing only approximately 14% of the total agricultural land, or about 9.6% of total provincial area, is in use for agricultural production. The remaining 86% of Savannakhet's agricultural land is not yet utilised for any purpose.

In February 2015, the Lao Government acknowledged that Vilabouly District, where the Sepon mine is located, had graduated from the list of 46 poorest districts in the Lao PDR (MMG, 2015). Vilabouly is also home to various ethnic groups such as Bru, Phu Tai, and Tai leu. From 46 villages in this area, our team randomly selected seven villages in Vilabouly district: Ban Vangyang, Namkeep, Ban Noonsomboon, Padong, Boungkham, Nongkadeang, and Ban Huay Suan.

Tab Klor (ทับคล้อ) and Khao Jed Luke (เขาเจ็ดลูก), Pijit, Thailand

Tab Klor and Khao Jed Luke are two districts in the west of Pijit province, Thailand. Originally, the key economic activities in this area were rice farming and animal husbandry. Tab Klor's original name was Tab Taklor (the place for Ta Klor tree), due to its fertile land and the high numbers of Ta Klor trees in this area. We selected Tab Klor and Khao Led Luke as the key research location in Thailand for two reasons: its economic contributions to Thailand through the mining industry, and its complex political situation, due to an ongoing conflict among various mining stakeholders in Thailand.

Figure 1. Research area in Lao PDR

This area is home to Chatree goldmine, operated by Akara Resources PCL. Akara is a subsidiary of Kingsgate Consolidated Limited, an Australian Securities Exchange (ASX) listed company. The Kingsgate Group held 48.2% of outstanding share capital as of June 30, 2013.

Chatree is 280km north of Bangkok and consists of 840 hectares. It commenced open-cut mining in 2001. Since commissioning of the Chatree Mining Complex in November 2001, and up to June 30, 2013, the mine produced over 1.3 million oz of gold and over 5.8 million oz of silver. In the year ended June 30, 2013, Akara resources produced 133K oz of gold at a total cash operating cost of US$767 per oz after royalty (Akara Resources, 2012).

Our research team randomly selected nine villages from the mining community in both districts as study sites in Thailand. All villages in this study are defined by the Thai Ministry of Interior as 'the Mining Villages', due to their vicinity to Chatree goldmine.

DATA COLLECTION, INTERVIEW, AND ANALYSIS

The feminist approach asks questions that place women's lives and those of other marginalised groups at the centre of inquiry (see Smith, 1987). From this standpoint, scholars have suggested that qualitative methods are more appropriate to feminist research, as they are best suited to revealing and understanding the experiences of individuals in contemporary society and adequately addressing their needs by allowing subjective knowledge

Figure 2. Research area in Thailand

(Depner, 1981), thus challenging partial accounts of the gendered lives of both women and men.

We are aware of the influence of power issues that can potentially distort the gender aspects among participants in this project. We tried to challenge the masculine assumptions of proper interviews that dominated the idea of management research Following Oakley's suggestion (1998) that, contrary to an objective, standardized, and detached approach to interviewing, the goal of finding out about people through interviewing was "best achieved when the relationship of interviewer and interviewee is non-hierarchical and when the interviewer is prepared to invest his or her own personal identity in the relationship", we carefully selected people who design, plan, and execute the interview process.

Interview questions and guides were co-developed by team members from all locations: Australia, Lao PDR and Thailand. They weretranslated into three languages. The interview questions were tested for validity prior to the fieldwork in all countries. The development of questions for this project was complex, due to the similar, yet diverse, nature of the Lao and Thai languages. When our team completed the questionnaire-design step, we invited three Thais and three Laotians to simplify the language, to ensure that our participants would not experience difficulty dealing with jargon or technical terms.

We selected interview as the main data-collection method because an interview is 'a conversation, whose purpose is to gather descriptions of the life-world of the interviewee' with respect to interpretation of the meanings of the 'described phenomena' (Marshall & Rossman, 2006, p.152.). An interview protocol was designed to encourage interviewees to participate in loosely guided conversations to facilitate the emergence of different themes.

In a similar vein, Neuman (2007) adds that an interview is an extendable conversation between partners that aims at acquiring in-depth information about a certain topic or subject, and through which a phenomenon could be interpreted in terms of the meaning interviewees bring to it. Accumulating such meanings can be done in various ways, of which one-on-one interviews are the most common. Besides one-on-one interviews, focus-group interviewing is also popular (Marshall & Rossman, 2006).

In Lao PDR, we selected participants from seven villages who are heavily influenced by the establishment of a mining company. All villagers who participated in this study were selected base on their involvement with various activities with either the mining company or Governmental agencies addressing mining issues. We conducted face-to-face interviews with 76 participants from these villages (including workers from the mining company, community leaders, family members of the workers and men and women from different ethnic groups). Sixty-two percent of the participants were women. Interviews were conducted in Lao, Bru and Phu Tai languages. The interviews were supported by our partners in Lao PDR (i.e., National University of Laos, Burnett Institute, and MMG LXML). All participants were purposefully selected by the research team members from Lao PDR. Snowball technique was the main technique to recruit participants from Lao PDR.

During the interview, we focused on their experiences in/with the mining company and their activities in the community. Our team also discussed participant selection with different community leaders in order to confirm the quality of the recruitment of research participants. All interviews were conducted at the community centre in the evening.

Focus groups were another method of data collection. This technique is appropriate for the nature of this research because we needed to explore people's opinions on a topic to understand what they think and why. More importantly, focus groups also provide rich and insightful data on people's motivations, choices and feelings.

We conducted two focus-group interviews with ten participants (five per group) who are the members of the local women's union and play different leadership roles in the community. All participants were selected based on their experiences in various projects related to women's empowerment.

In Thailand, we interviewed 43 participants from 9 villages located in the mining area in the Tab Klor and Khao Jed Luke Districts. We selected workers from the mining company, community leaders, family members of workers from the mining company, and policy makers from the local province. Sixty-eight percent of the participants were women. All interviews were conducted at the participants' respective households and offices.

Before each interview in both countries, all publicly available documents related to the company's CSR programmes and gender policies were read and analysed to provide additional information on how each MNC presented itself with regard to its CSR and gender approaches and activities. The researchers focused on company-created documents including their websites, company reports, codes of conduct/ethics, performance indicators and case studies. These were used to prepare interviews and to support interview data. Each interview lasted approximately 40 minutes and was conducted face-to-face at each organisation's premises.

Participants were asked to discuss three broad topics: impacts of company's actions and policies on CSR and gender, gender and employment, and relationships among company issues (i.e., environment, health, skills) and mining stakeholders. Issues of validity and reliability were addressed at the data-collection stage by using digital recordings and notes taken directly following each interview, which included nonverbal cues or other pertinent information on the interview process itself (Yin, 1998).

During the interview, as suggested by Holmwood (1995) that there might be the ethical dilemmas involved in conducting research with disadvantaged or marginalized women, as well as larger epistemological issues involved in attempting to "know" others, we carefully employed students who do not have personal relationship with anyone in the local area to collect the data with academic staff from three major Universities in Lao PDR and Thailand. In order to be fair for all participants in this study, we discouraged personal friendship while collecting the data since it can potentially influence their private and personal aspects of lives.

The researchers transcribed the data together. They adopted abstraction (Clarkson, 1995) to analyse the data, so themes were grouped by similarity of ideas, allowing movement from concrete to more general and theoretically useful themes. These higher-order themes were then further abstracted using axial coding to link categories hierarchically, so that more general themes included relevant subthemes (Grant, Hardy, Oswick, & Putnam, 2004). This resulted in fewer higher-order categories and their relevant subcategories, for which respective dimensions could be identified and analysed (Yin, 2004).

In addition, various other sources were used to supplement the fieldwork data, including archival records, social-responsibility reports, information from corporate websites, newspaper clips and other publicly available social information. The data collected from the research were transcribed and thematically analysed. Critical reflection on the research process, the responses—especially why certain stories were recounted rather than others—and the complex interpersonal dynamics offered some further insights into the subject matter.

REFERENCES

Akara Resources. (2012). *Sustainability report 2012, annual report.* Retrieved from http://www.akararesources.com/en/sustainability/cg/sd-report

Clarkson, M. (1995). A stakeholder framework for analyzing and evaluating corporate social performance. *Academy of Management Review, 20*(1), 92–117. doi:10.5465/amr.1995.9503271994

Depner, C. (1981). *Towards the further development of feminist psychology.* Paper presented at the mid-winter conference of the Association for Women in Psychology, Boston, MA.

Grant, D., Hardy, C., Oswick, C., & Putnam, L. (Eds.). (2004). *The Sage handbook of organisational discourse.* Thousand Oaks, CA: Sage.

Holmwood, J. (1995). Feminism and epistemology: What kind of successor science? *Sociology, 29*(3), 411–428. doi:10.1177/0038038595029003003

Marshall, C., & Rossman, G. B. (2006). *Designing qualitative research* (4th ed.). Thousand Oaks, CA: Sage.

MMG. (2015). *MMG sustainability report 2015.* Retrieved from http://www.mmg.com/en/Investors-and-Media/News/2016/05/11/MMG-Releases-2015-Sustainability-Report.aspx?pn=7&backitem=BA5603A202CE4D1E848FABA9D1339247

Neuman, W. L. (2007). *Social research methods: Qualitative and quantitative approaches* (6th ed.). Boston: Pearson.

Oakley, A. (1998). Gender, methodology and people's ways of knowing: Some problems with feminism and the paradigm debate in social science. *Sociology, 32*(4), 707–731. doi:10.1177/0038038598032004005

Smith, D. (1987). *The everyday world as problematic: a feminist sociology.* Northeastern University Press.

Yin, R. K. (1998). The abridged version of case study research. In L. Bickman & D. J. Rog (Eds.), *Handbook of applied social research methods* (pp. 229–259). Thousand Oaks, CA: Sage Publications.

Yin, R. K. (2004). *The case study anthology.* Thousand Oaks, CA: Sage.

Chapter 4
Gender, CSR, and Mining:
Perspectives From Lao PDR

ABSTRACT

This chapter presents the key findings on how the mining industry and MNCs influence various aspects of life and wellbeing of women in Lao PDR. The study shows that mining MNCs can provide various opportunities for women. Mining MNCs have clung to the narrow compliance-based view of CSR for certain periods of time, due to the management system and corporate policies. They seem to focus on economic activities to empower women and promote the concept of gender equality. The data supports the contention that avoiding the potential detrimental effects that mining MNCs can have on fragile ecosystems, gender inequality, and local social issues should be made a priority. Recently, however, mining MNCs have tended to shift their actions to sustainable economic and skill development in Lao, due to their understanding of local contexts. The results also show that opportunities provided by mining MNCs can create long-term benefits to various members of the community including family of the miners, suppliers, trans-border and transnational workers, and women from low socioeconomic backgrounds.

DOI: 10.4018/978-1-5225-3811-0.ch004

INTRODUCTION

Lao PDR is a small and landlocked developing country in Southeast Asia with a population of approximately 5 million. It has a land area of 236,800 km2, stretching more than 1,700 km from north to south. The country borders Cambodia, China, Myanmar, Thailand and Vietnam. It also comprises more than 49 ethnic groups from 4 ethnolinguistic families with distinctive cultures and values.

The Lao Government has set clear economic and development objectives. Through foreign direct investment, the mining industry is perceived as one mechanism to liberate the country from the group of Least Developed Countries (LDCs) by the year 2020 (Department of Mines [DOM], 2008). As reported by the International Monetary Fund (IMF) in 2010, the lack of information on socioeconomic characteristics of the poor in Lao, particularly women and people from certain ethnic groups, can lead to less effective planning in empowering women in the community (High, 2010). The alternative is to focus on how mining MNCs can utilise their resources to empower women through their CSR activities.

Given the impact of mining companies in Lao PDR, the dimension of social engagement and building relationships with various other stakeholders in the community is particularly interesting in the context of local communities. This chapter reports different dimensions of how mining companies and the industry influence women in Lao PDR from the community's perspectives.

WOMEN AND EMPLOYMENT

The Vilabouly community comprises members from Laos, countries outside of Laos and ethnic minorities. While we were working in the field, we observed that the major occupations in Vilabouly include mining-related work, the agricultural sector and small and medium enterprises (SMEs). Prior to the advent of the mining industry in the community, most people worked on the farm and in the forest (DOM, 2008). Some may have continued their work when the mining industry was introduced to the community. Some changed their career from the agricultural sector to mining. The relationship between mining and women in the community is a close one.

From the interviews with various members of the Vilabouly community, we learnt that the mining industry creates tremendous economic opportunities for women in Vilabouly and those who migrate to work and reside in Vilabouly. Women can engage in various types of work and economic opportunities in the mining industry. From the community's perspective, the CSR programmes of the mining company operating in Laos provide a mechanism to compensate for the social and environmental costs associated with mining. These costs are usually associated with environmental impact, higher food and housing costs, relocation and social impacts from an increase in the number of workers living in the area.

When it comes to employment by mining MNC, the company clearly understands that mining is traditionally a male-dominated industry, and it may be difficult to attract and retain women to work in the industry. In their recruitment and employment policies, the company encourages women to apply for various positions from the operation of heavy machinery, management and administration to supporting roles in the mine. The goal of this approach to gender equity is to minimise differences between women and men so that women can compete as equals.

To encourage Lao women in the industry, the company must guide them toward understanding their roles, values and contributions to the organisation. This is important for the company to play the role of promoter to encourage women in the organisation.

Some strategies include leadership-development programmes for women, introducing flexible work practises, open discussion of career paths with all members in the organisation (both men and women), and assertiveness training for men and women. It is also stated in the sustainability report of a mining company in Lao PDR that targeting women to manage the organisation is one of the key business strategies of the company.

Encouraging women to actively participate in various company activities is an effective approach because it convinces women to believe in their power and contributions. Participants from the company confirmed that because Lao women are usually in a disadvantaged position in the workplace compared to Lao men, encouraging women through formal and informal corporate channels points to explicit attention to women's needs and perspectives. Traditional ways of discouraging women in the mining industry may persist. Hereafter, it is important for mining MNCs to make sure that men also play roles in encouraging women in the corporation.

Mining MNCs in this study also focus on removing structural barriers that impede women's learning new skills, promotion, and leading the organisation. The company also focuses on strategies to provide equal opportunities for both men and women. Some local tradition may promote the idea of gender-specific roles at work and discourage equal opportunity for women. Managers from this mining company clearly pointed out that, unlike men, Lao women in the organisation may perceive some difficulties in progressing to its upper levels due to lack of proper skills, training and time to upgrade their qualifications.

When Lao women work with male foreigners in the international mining-industry environment, women may feel inferior to their male counterparts. This circumstance can impede women pursuing leadership roles and positions in the organisation, since most managerial positions are dominated by male foreigners, mostly English speaking and educated in the West. Managers from the company agreed that statements or messages that the organisation promotes equal opportunities must be frequently communicated though various communication channels.

The mining company in this study also recognises women's primary caregiver role as a structural barrier to their advancement. The majority of women still work in supportive roles such as cleaning, cooking and basic administrative roles. Mining MNCs agree that they need to promote equal-opportunity policies for women by eliminating traditional ideas that women can only do certain jobs. Structural barriers include the lack of gender-inclusive policy, organisational support, or representation of women within the organisation.

Participants from both mining MNCs pointed out that appropriate recruitment and promotion procedures have been implemented to increase opportunities for women to work in leadership positions, laboratory and science, as well as on mining survey. Most women who are newly recruited are aware of equal access to jobs, benefits, and services for all employees and prospective employees in the workplace. Obviously, both mining MNCs are aware of the glass-ceiling effect and try to minimise structural barriers that impede women's growth. This point is not that dissimilar from a report by Kemp (2012) that the implementation of gender equality in Lao PDR is often inhibited due to the persistence of traditional practices and women's lack of awareness of their own rights.

When we look at company policies, equal opportunity is about ensuring that women have equal access to the rewards and opportunities available in the workplace. A manager from a mining company in Lao PDR stated that women must be treated with respect and not be subject to discrimination or harassment.

Both MNCs in this study identify equal opportunity as an organising principle and process that shapes social structure, identities and knowledge. The focus is then on different sets of gendering processes, including formal practises and policies; informal work practises; and symbols and images that express, legitimise and reinforce gendered divisions in organisations.

MINING, CSR AND ECONOMIC ISSUES FOR WOMEN

When discussing economic-development issues, mining MNCs in Laos have clung to the narrow compliance-based view of CSR. Most corporate representatives seem to focus on economic activities to alleviate poverty as a direct response to women in the community.

Recently, however, mining MNCs have tended to shift their actions to sustainable economic development in the host countries. All companies in this study enables economic development by promoting opportunities for employment and skills improvement, creating fair trade systems in local supply chains, providing more technical support for girls and women, and capacity-building activities through public-private investment. These economic CSR activities promote higher standard economic systems among women in the community.

The obvious economic opportunities for women in Vilabouly include mining-related work, business with the mining company, business for workers of the company, skill-building programmes by mining companies, and various capacity-building programmes for the community. Working for the mining company in Vilabouly is perceived as a high-status job for women since it involves big multinational corporations. Most women who work in the mining industry state that employment with the company provides not only income but also opportunities to engage in various company activities. Economic independence with mining as its source is clearly important as an ideology to promote equity.

Participants from Ban Vanyang, Padong and Huaysuan are of Blu ethnic background and mentioned that sociolinguistic issues may limit their employment in the mining company. They also mentioned the impact of land entitlement on their lives. When agriculture activities are disrupted by mining activities—because agricultural land is no longer available or soil and water sources are depleted or polluted—women start to worry about their future income and work harder, longer, or farther from home to earn a decent income.

Certain limitations remain of concern among women in this study. Most women must actively participate in professional development and skill-building activities of mining MNCs. They seek opportunities to be able to play different roles in the organisation, although such opportunities can be limited for women.

Most women in this study have been in the same roles, and some of them are eager to play different roles at the workplace. Skills training and professional development will be important mechanisms to promote the ability of women in mining MNCs to upgrade their professional status and experiences. The company also mentioned the village-development funds. In each project, small grants of up to US$15,000 per year were then provided to the village. Participants mentioned that facilities from the funds such as the construction of latrines, roads, schools, fish ponds and village meeting halls are useful for women in the community.

Women in the mining industry also refer to economic empowerment activities that are the results of a mining establishment in the community. Activities such as vocational skills training, basic educational supports and professional-development programmes, microfinance schemes, and village funds are perceived as important ongoing activities for women.

WOMEN AND GENDER-SPECIFIC ROLES

Male-dominated culture also structures the day-to-day work and job design in large-scale mines. For instance, mining is performed in routinely long hours of work where part-time or flexible work practises for workers to integrate and balance their work and personal or family life are severely limited. Where flexible work practises are available, there is limited take-up, so the full-time working week is the norm. This is a key barrier to workers with caring and earning responsibilities, predominantly women.

Women in Vilabouly seem to have differing views on the traditional male-dominated culture of this industry. Most women are comfortable playing the role of family leader, with strong support from their husbands and other family members. Women who earn from the mining industry seem to gain status from family and community. Some of them have switched roles with their husbands. Some women who work in the mining industry expressed views that, due to time commitments at work, their husbands must play the role of house husband. They also have equal say in family financial issues. Family members must agree upon these changes in roles.

With economic-empowerment activities from the industry, women can participate more in political roles in the community. We witnessed a female village head, a female head of the village funds, and women representatives on the village committee.

While the increase in female participation is of benefit to the economy, in many cases it has led to difficulties combining the demands of work, family and community life. Balancing and integrating these competing demands primarily falls into the domain of women as a social practise.

Some women may be reluctant to switch roles and must do both 'traditional work' and 'full-time employment'. This can create low self-esteem. Women in the mining industry still struggle with expectations from their family, their husband's families, and the community. At the same time, they need to commit themselves to the full-time job.

WOMEN AND ACTIVITIES BY MINING COMPANY

The mining company is an important member of the community. Apart from economic activities, other sociopolitical activities can impact women in Vilabouly.

Through their CSR schemes, the company can improve access to resources among women of various ethnic backgrounds in the community. Funding and various other microfinance schemes are perceived as positive initiatives by the mining industry. It improves access to other key resources such as health services, education and training. The focus-group meeting with women revealed that poverty and desperation to support family members compel women in the mining areas to engage in various activities of the mining company. Their intention is to earn more to support their family members. If done correctly, CSR can be one solution to improving their living conditions.

Some women suggested that relevance of CSR activities should be discussed among mining stakeholders Most activities are seen as generic and not relevant to women's needs. The absence and underrepresentation of women in decision-making and agenda-setting forums by the mining company, when it comes to various issues such as recruitment and benefits for staff, often mean that the rights, needs, and interests of women in Vilabouly are neglected and not prioritised, while women's skills, experience and knowledge remain underutilised.

In addition, a range of initiatives has been implemented that encompasses all villages in close proximity to the mining operations. These include health-education programmes, village clean-water supply infrastructure utilising solar technology and village savings and loan schemes. All programmes have been designed to mitigate dependency on funding from outside the community as soon as feasible, at least by the time the mine closes. The life of mining and its relationship with the economic status of Vilabouly is an important issue among women in this study. They raised a concern about what the future of Vilabouly will be after the end of the mining industry. As the mine's footprint grows, land will be lost to operational requirements, but many new jobs are unlikely to be created to offset the loss of land. Women are worried about losing their incomes and benefits from the industry. More importantly, most of them do not have professional skills that will lead them to future employment. It is speculated that mining will be finished within five to seven years. Thus, men and women in Vilabouly must be ready for their future directions.

WOMEN AND HEALTH

Health is complex, the result of a raft of socioeconomic determinants. When it comes to health, women in Vilabouly are impacted by mining in all aspects of life. The women are key to reversing disadvantage in their communities. Hiring women has greater welfare impact on families; they spend income in ways that increase child health and well-being. Many health issues faced by women in the mining sector are due to stigma, discrimination and their low status in the community.

Many women in Vilabouly report close-to-equal employment in the local mine and capacity-building/training opportunities to men, although they want more skills to transfer to other future employment. Some women find the rigid nature of this work, and its strenuous nature, detrimental to physical and mental health demands; others were less stressed than they would be in other less reliable occupations such as farming.

Household income is generally managed by women, with girl's education and health taking priority in expenditures, and with some saving for the future. Women's social status overall has increased.

Environmental degradation was a concern for women's health, as was social change for a minority that includes a husband's alcohol consumption (rarely associated with violence against women). Most women in this study admitted that they ponder the future of the community and themselves. Environmental impacts from mining industry increase their level of stress since they are not certain about the future after the closure of mining industry and the lack of fertile land. They may have to migrate to Vientiane or other towns in order to survive the next chapter of life.

WOMEN AND EDUCATION

Education provision is certainly important among men and women in Vilabouly. Apart from education opportunities that come with consistent income from the mining industry, equity in education can be supported by the establishment of the mining industry in the community.

Most women in this study expressed their desire to support both boys and girls in their family in reaching their education potential. They have learnt from the past that education equity will promote the access of girls and women to resources and active participation in various other societal and political issues in the community. One compelling statement from a participation form from this study shows how important vocational training can lead to a long-term solution for women from all backgrounds in Lao PDR.

We hope the company provides women with a range of training such as accounting, management, and English language so women can easily find work when the mine closes.

Vocational training programmes provided by the mining company through its CSR scheme, such as weaving, farming or design, are perceived as sustainable community development. Some women in the community expressed that they also need to participate in different types of educational and skill-building programmes, such as foreign-language training, accounting, entrepreneurial skills, and marketing. The concern regards the future of their family and kids after the closure of the mine. Education and training will help women in the community to sustain their equitable roles with men in the community (Oxfam, 2017).

Another important aspect of women, education and mining is the role and power of the mining company to educate and promote understanding on issues related to the industry. Most women in this study seem to agree that it is the company's responsibility to engage men and women in the process of learning about the impact and development of the industry. Through partnerships with government and civil society in the community, they can ensure that benefits of mining extend beyond the life of the mine itself, so that the mining industry has a strong impact on the natural environment, climate change and economic, gender and social capital.

REFERENCES

Department of Mines. (2008). *Annual report and presentation on Mining Activities in Lao PDR*. Available at: http://www.dmr.go.th/download/lao_thai56/pdf_dat/Mining%20activities%20in%20Lao%20pdr%20.pdf

High, H. (2010). Laos: Crisis and resource contestation. *Southeast Asian Affairs, 2010*(1), 153–161. doi:10.1355/SEAA10J

Oxfam. (2017). *Position paper on gender justice and the extractive industries*. Available at https://www.oxfam.org.au/wp-content/uploads/2017/04/EI_and_GJ_position_paper_v.15_FINAL_03202017_green_Kenny.pdf

Chapter 5
Gender, CSR, and Mining:
Perspectives From Thailand

ABSTRACT

This chapter focuses on the impact of mining MNCs and the industry on women in Thailand. Similar to most cases of mining communities in developing countries, the results show various socioeconomic impacts of mining MNCs in Thailand. They include work and economic opportunities for women, political roles and participation for women, and health issues, which seemed prominent among women who participated in this study. Local and international environmental groups have become increasingly involved in mining disputes with the Thai community that participated in this study. Meanwhile, local communities have become more concerned about shouldering all the negative impacts of mining but receiving few of the benefits. This is especially the case because capital-intensive large mining operations generate only a fraction of the jobs for certain groups of people. This study shows that employment policies of mining MNCs have affected the geographic distribution of benefits and costs. The influx of new migrants from Bangkok or other major cities also puts great strains on the existing social and economic infrastructure. It is essential that some mechanisms exist to ensure an orderly expansion of activities and provision of services by mining MNCs in Thailand.

DOI: 10.4018/978-1-5225-3811-0.ch005

INTRODUCTION

Achieving gender equality requires the engagement of women and men, girls and boys. It is everyone's responsibility. (Ban Ki-Moon)

Gender inequality in Thailand is rooted in history and based in the family unit. To a lesser degree, it is the result of culturally rooted social policy (Hansatit, 2014). Men have long been seen as the leader of families and communities in Thai society, and are expected to be the breadwinners as well. Moreover, since most Thai parents felt that sons were born to a superior role, they tended to provide them with the best education possible (Hansatitt, 2014). Girls were traditionally left ignorant or barely literate because the parents believed their ultimate goal was to marry and become homemakers. Therefore, other knowledge and skills beyond that necessary for family life was neglected for girls. This path is still followed today in many Thai families, especially in rural areas (Hansatit, 2014). Recently, the World Economic Forum (2015) put Thailand in 60th place out of 145 countries measured in its Gender Gap Index .

In this study, we observed a mining community located in the Thai rural area. Tab Klor and Khao Jed Luke are two districts in Pijit province, Thailand, where we investigated the CSR impacts of mining

Although the mine has been the main source of income for most community members in the Tab Klor and Khao Jed Luke areas, there has long been an ongoing conflict among various community members and the company. The Chatree mine, operated by Akara Resources, Public Company Limited, a subsidiary of the Australian operator Kingsgate, has been the target of environmental protests over alleged contamination of nearby villages. Interestingly, the majority of participants in this study are women who may have direct or indirect experiences with the impacts of the mining company in the community.

We focus on four aspects as key themes: employment, gender and society, health and environment and political roles of women in the mining community.

WOMEN AND EMPLOYMENT

Women residing in Tab Klor and Khao Jed Luke districts work in various industries. The majority work in the rice field and mentioned land-entitlement problems. When the mining industry was established in the area, some of them or their family members gained employment from the company. Employment by a mining MNC in this area has also been perceived as an economic opportunity for some women who previously had no technical skills and could not find employment in any other sectors. This applies in particular to women who had neither owned a piece of land nor mastered any work skills.

Similar to most mining MNCs in various developing countries, the recruitment process of the company is questionable for a number of women in the community. Mining MNCs tend to focus on formal educational qualifications when recruiting new staff. This is not realistic for most rural areas in Thailand where education is not easily afforded by those at the bottom of the socioeconomic hierarchy. Although women show interest in working in the industry, most of them are limited by lack of educational qualifications, experiences and skills. Local women addressed the lack of proper education as the key impediment to women thriving in this industry. Lack of education can be seen as the old Thai way of thinking that family resources should be spent on education for boys instead of girls. Women also lack opportunities to access skill development for employment.

Most local women who work in the mining industry work in the traditional roles for women, such as cleaning, cooking, administration and office roles. Although the company has tried to promote various roles in the company, women in the community may not actively participate in the process. Roles such as engineering, machine operations or business management are dominated by men, though increasing numbers of women can be confirmed.

Women from the community also see employment in the mining industry as an opportunity for both men and women to survive the current economy in Thailand. Compared to employment in other sectors, mining can provide employees with high economic returns. Most women also openly discussed the concept of the relationship between sustainable income from the mining company and family future (e.g., education for their children, a new house, future investment). To them, income from the mining company is not only current gain but also the guarantee for the future.

Equitable employment is also mentioned by women as appropriate company practise. Some women would like to see equity among people of all backgrounds in the areas of gender, education, age and location, with respect to working in this industry in Thailand. They see employment opportunities as a means to relocate to live with family in Pijit and Pitsanuloke provinces.

Employment by the mining company in Thailand is not perceived as CSR. For the community where the company is located, employment is an economic activity from which the mining company and the community mutually benefit. The role of the company in gender equality remains unclear since there is no clear policy on women or women's employment.

WOMEN AND GENDER-SPECIFIC ROLES

From the interviews with various members of both districts, we learnt that the mining industry may create some changes in gender roles in the community. A vast majority of women we interviewed still prefer to work in agriculture, stay at home, and look after family. This traditional view of women's roles in Thailand remains common in this society. However, some women take active roles in political engagement in the community.

Due to conflicts among some community members, NGOs, and the mining company, some women lead the community and actively play political roles. They have been engaging with other community members, national and international media and government. They expressed that being female helps them to use different approaches to negotiate with different stakeholders in the mining community.

Women who actively engage in political efforts in the mining industry advocate for environmental issues, health impacts of the industry, and political relations among industry and government.

Leading the community and other women in the politics of mining is not of interest to men for a number of reasons. Most women expressed that men are too busy with work commitments. Most men and women who work in the mining industry also said that the issue is too sensitive, and they do not want to risk their career by involving themselves in the politics of mining. Women who lead the community and advocate for social issues also perceive that men are less active than women in advocacy for equity and societal issues in the community.

Instead of playing the passive role of mother or family caretaker, some women from Tab Klor also engage actively with the mining company and other women in the community to create business opportunities. Most of them understand ways to access financial and technical resources from the local government, the mining company, and educational institutions. Through funding and microfinance schemes from the company, some women can create occupational groups for women in the community in such activities as sewing and farming.

WOMEN, HEALTH AND ENVIRONMENT

This issue has been ongoing in the community, with different views on health and environmental impacts of the mining industry there.

Some community members reported the impacts of mining operations on water, air and noise quality in the community. Quality of water was mentioned as the major concern, among other environmental impacts of mining. Although the company has supplied the community with water for consumption and general uses, villagers still raise their concerns about its long-term impacts and ongoing health problems.

Women who work in the agricultural sector also raise concerns about mining impacts on land fertility. They are worried that mining operations may impact the quality of land and rain. If some negative impacts persist, young women may need to find other work and migrate to Bangkok or nearby areas.

Most women we interviewed expressed their view that the lack of female participation in the governance system may have led to current health and environmental problems in the community. The majority of leading roles in the local government are occupied by males, with some females in supporting roles.

The fact that the mining operation was shut down and inspected by the military government in January 2015, due to suspension of its environmental impact from the operation of the company. In 2018, the company was charged by the Thai department of investigation. They include illegitimately acquiring land-rights documents for forestland, of encroaching on a highway and of encroaching on forestland.

This issue creates uncertainty among members of the mining community, including women. As mentioned, the community is divided into opponents and supporters of the mining industry; thus, views on this issue among women can be unclear, different, and segregated. After repeated conflicts between mine operators and locals, the National Council for Peace and Order decided in 2016 to exercise Section 44 to suspend operations of all gold mines nationwide (The Nations, 2018).

In sum, the common health-impact issues among women in this study include the leakage of substances such as arsenic and manganese into the water; concerns regarding air pollution; skin rashes; noise; chemical substances in the ground; and reproductive health. These issues are routinely reported by women in the community. Most women in this study also raised concerns about long-term health impacts on women since the relationship between the mining operations and disease remains unclear.

WOMEN AND POLITICAL ROLES

This issue has been ongoing in the community. There are different views on the politics of health and environmental impacts of the mining industry in the community, some of which rose to the surface while we were conducting this research.

The Thai government's Department of Primary Industries and Mines ordered a 30-day suspension of activities by Akara Resources. The suspension followed a protracted dispute between Akara and local villagers. The locals claimed—and this was voiced predominantly by women—that they had been adversely affected by the mine's activities.

Despite the concerns raised by villagers, Akara continued to issue environmental-impact studies that failed to address their concerns. However, when the Thai government assessed the mine's impacts on environment and health, arsenic and manganese were found to exceed acceptable levels in 282 villagers living near Kingsgate's Chatree gold mine in Pijit Province.

Female participants who had been actively engaging in political activity raised an important concern that women in the mining community could play more influential roles than their male counterparts, because the political consequences of the mining industry are related to their family. They feel that they need to engage with the mining company, political leaders, and other members in the community. The key concern is how women actively participate in the decision-making on use of resources by the mining industry. Akara injects 37 million Thai baht (A\$1,465,011) into funds for 27 villages close to the mine, but generally places spending of funds in the hands of community leaders. Although villagers themselves would dearly like to participate in this decision-making process, in practise most still defer to village heads and local administrators, so these funds tend to be tightly controlled by the heads of villages, all male, and those closest to them. Additionally, the company provides disparate financial support to different villages. When resources are accessible, those who have a say in their utilisation are mostly men of relatively high socioeconomic status.

Despite the current outcry, all villagers in our study said they wanted the mine in their community. Yet, they want a company that is trustworthy and systematically demonstrates strong commitment to environmental protection.

REFERENCES

Hansatit, P. (2014). *A study on gender inequality in Thailand: Career experience of Thai female managers* (DBA thesis). Southern Cross University, Lismore, Australia.

The Nations. (2018). *Mine boss reports over encroachment*. Retrieved from https://www.bangkokpost.com/news/general/1530062/mine-boss-reports-over-encroachment

The World Economic Forum. (2015). *Global Gender Gap Index*. Retrieved from http://reports.weforum.org/global-gender-gap-report-2015/the-global-gender-gap-index-2015/

Chapter 6
Mining and Women:
Business and Community

ABSTRACT

Whilst CSR is significant for nearly all MNCs, CSR activities have been limited to certain activities and focus areas. In developing countries such as Thailand and Laos, CSR activities focus on economic and social development in many forms. However, we learn from this study that the CSR movement would advance if different types of MNCs actively participated in various socioeconomic activities in host countries. In most developing countries in Asia, such as Thailand, Laos, Vietnam, or Cambodia, CSR by MNCs is concerned with the integration of environmental, social, and economic considerations into business strategies and practices. However, this is not as simple as it sounds. Some argue that CSR is beneficial to MNCs that do integrate it into their everyday practices; others say that it is only a way for MNCs to promote new products and features. This chapter argues that although a feminist epistemology of mining would query the representation of women as 'victims of mining', there are various ways for mining MNCs to empower and promote women in the mining community. The authors discuss lessons from Laos and Thailand in order to stimulate a rethinking of mining itself, as an area representing an environment, which is both feminine and masculine.

DOI: 10.4018/978-1-5225-3811-0.ch006

INTRODUCTION

The most successful companies are those that integrate sustainability into their core businesses. (Jim Owens, CEO, Caterpillar)

This book argues that we can move away from the traditional masculine norm of the mining industry, well-explained by Lahiri-Dutt (2011, p.195):

The masculinity of popular images of the miner is ingrained in the corporate machismo of the globalised industry, controlled by shareholders based in the global North. Explorers' adventures and heroism fuel this machismo; vivid accounts of the first sightings of a famous ore body turn discoverers into cultural heroes who wander across usually hostile landscapes until they find the mineral deposit. Such corporate fuelled hyper-machismo is common in representations of mining entrepreneurs or overpaid executives which are found widely in popular media.

Business involvement in community issues is not uncommon. Communities face various issues in which business organisations can play various roles to show their commitment to the community. In this project, we have learnt that mining MNC motivations for addressing developmental issues, such as gender equality and poverty alleviation, could arise because of either a strong ethical commitment to their stakeholders in the community, or their strong practical interest in the issues of host countries.

Mining MNCs in this study demonstrated both old and new schools of CSR strategies and implementation. Both mining MNCs in this study are large scale and complex in terms of operations and people involved in the organisations. The nature of large-scale mining MNCs is to employ primarily male workforces, having more men than women in management and various other jobs and functions. They may make a series of gendered impacts on local communities. Where mining companies act as development agencies, their programmes may also cause further social change.

In many cases in both countries, we affirmed that CSR in mining has now moved beyond the occasional philanthropy of the past, where donations or the building of infrastructure required only minimal interaction with local communities. Many large-scale mining companies now have departments dedicated to community development and sophisticated policies for community engagement and development programmes. Working closely with different stakeholders in the community has become the priority for mining MNCs.

The business cases for CSR seem to focus on a wide range of potential economic benefits. These include financial performance and profitability, reduced operating cost, long-term financial gains for companies, employees' welfare, increased staff commitment and involvement, enhanced capacity to innovate, good relations with government and communities, better risk and crisis management, enhanced reputation and brand value and, of course, the development of closer links with customers and greater awareness of their needs.

The subject academic debate entails those critics who question the greater attention paid to the CSR community initiatives in the application of shareholder funds, without regard for the likely effect on the business's financial profits or the organisation's future opportunities for research, innovation and expansion. For instance, Kapstein (2001) reiterates the ideas of neoclassic economist Milton Friedman (1962) that business's only social responsibility is to use its resources to engage in activities designed to increase its profit, as long as it engages in open and free competition without deception or fraud. Friedman's (1962) concept of the business and societal relationship was centred strictly on business producing the needed goods and services at prices people in the society could afford. In his work, Friedman (1962) identifies a departure from this business role amounting to spending someone else's money and placing the firm at a competitive disadvantage. Friedman also questions whether managers are competent to engage in social issues and saw no reason this group of individuals should carry out the role of government in the society (Kapstein, 2001).

Empirical research on MNCs and their behaviour has been limited particularly to developing and emerging economies. The focus is on how and why MNCs engage in CSR, and if their CSR strategies in developing countries are aligned to their global commitment to sustainable development. More importantly, studies (e.g., Lee & Faff, 2009; Pimpa, 2013) confirm that good CSR practises can positively impact an MNC's management process and lead to numerous managerial benefits that move beyond benefits for its shareholders.

The final chapter presents a summary of challenges for business organisations (such as MNCs) when they attempt to engage the community in their CSR programmes. CSR and inclusivity of women will be the focal points for discussion in this chapter.

THE INCLUSIVITY OF WOMEN AND CSR STRATEGIES BY MINING MNCS

We have witnessed the transformation of women in modern Southeast Asia. It is not uncommon to see female leaders in governmental, for-profit and nonprofit sectors. Social and economic changes influence women to move beyond traditional housework or childbearing. The emergence and establishment of the mining industry in the region create countless opportunities for all community members, including women and girls.

We learnt from the project that social stakeholders in both countries are key drivers for mining MNCs to engage in various activities leading to women's empowerment. Having women from various backgrounds involved in activities such as microfinance management, village banks, or skill-development activities can positively engage various stakeholders, including MNCs, in the host countries. The involvement of women in CSR approaches prominent among mining MNCs in both countries include communitarian, integrative and engagement initiatives.

In the Thai and Lao cultural context, community plays an important role in political and social stances. All three motivating factors reported in this study—management of relationships with mining stakeholders, organisational commitment and social licence to operate—are strongly related to the communitarian approach.

The integration with the community is related to nearly all aspects of CSR by mining MNCs in Thailand and Laos. It reflects concern for both self and others. Mining MNCs understand that they must promote synergy and work toward the development and achievement of individual and group goals. More importantly, giving back as a key Buddhist concept can occur for the benefit of their community. Being community-centric, focusing on involving women in various aspects of their activities, can also protect mining MNCs from some common criticisms, such as being profit oriented, exploitation of resources in the host countries and economic imperialism.

The concept of social licence to operate in host countries is also prominent among mining MNCs. We learnt from the project that social legitimacy and trust can help mining MNCs to obtain long-term social licence to operate in the Thai and Laotian context. Trust is an important element in conducting CSR strategies from the Thai cultural perspective. We also argue that trust comes from shared experiences among various stakeholders in the mining community.

The challenge for mining MNCs is to go beyond transactions with the community and create opportunities to collaborate, work together and generate the shared experiences within which trust can grow. Obviously, there is often considerable complexity involved in gaining and maintaining 'social licence', but properly prepared and supported, the challenges created by such circumstance can usually be overcome.

Mining MNCs in both countries realise that women play various roles in the community. They start to focus on ways to empower women. Economic empowerment is an obvious CSR strategy that leads to better quality of life among women. Mining MNCs also promote women-led SMEs that can flourish in the mining supply chain. Women can also be promoted through various social mechanisms such as education and skills development, health promotion, human rights, governance and leadership in the international mining industry.

In the context of business, society and women, all mining MNCs in this study characterised their CSR practises on social development, including empowerment of women through various aspects, with phrases such as 'open', 'sharing', 'mutual respect', 'active partnership' and 'long-term' commitment to the community. Most of the partners include key male and female leaders from the community in the host countries as part of the plan to empower women. Examples of key persons in the community who can support CSR strategies for income generation programmes for women are head of the village, key persons from the municipality council, school principals and teachers, Buddhist monks and head of the women's union.

We also learnt the pattern of relationship between MNC approaches to poverty alleviation and influence from regulatory and community stakeholders. In fact, we can assume that there is a high degree of interdependence between the MNC's competitive environment, policies and actions, as regulatory and community stakeholders can influence public opinion, demands and expectations. Also, they have power to channel valuable resources toward or away from MNCs.

Data from mining MNCs in this study conform to a high number of issues from the poverty-evaluation framework. Most MNCs appear willing to state active commitment only if others in their sector do so as well. It might be suggested that MNCs fear that because of their involvement in poverty alleviation, they might lose out to others that do not have a strong policy, and/or that claim to be active but fail to enforce it.

FINAL REMARKS

While ideologies of human rights, gender equity and the elimination of discrimination underpin most large multinational corporations' employment policies, counterideologies of gender equity often prevail in practise (Grosser & Moon, 2015). Most mining multinational corporations have been striving to adopt business ideologies and developmental practises that promote equity among men and women. However, it is reported that women in the mining industry still struggle to work at a similar level to men (Mercier & Gier, 2007).

Our project confirms that several social factors can be attributed to gender disengagement practises among stakeholders in the mining industry, such as mining MNCs, local authorities, community, NGOs and local government agencies. The failure to promote engagement among these stakeholders and existing unstable and weak national institutions leads to gender-based disadvantages.

There is evidence of increasingly effective and sophisticated developmental activities on gender equity by mining MNCs, but no clear understanding of various approaches they have adopted. Due to their significant economic and social roles, we must understand how mining MNCs promote gender equity and integrate women into their operations. More importantly, factors promoting women in international business organisations such as mining MNCs must be comprehended in order to support long-term strategies to empower and promote women in this male-dominated industry.

As gender equity in international business is a prominent issue, it has been difficult for all stakeholders, including mining MNCs to claim ignorance of their contribution in this area. Some may claim that mining MNCs should be proactive in positive contribution to 5he host countries. This has not led to constraints on mining MNCs that would cause them to behave according to norms that would be conducive to mitigating this important issue in the host and home countries.

The results of this project carry important implications for stakeholders in the international mining industry. Policy makers and practitioners from mining MNCs address eclectic approaches that can be implemented to promote women in the mining industry. This study highlights different approaches adopted by mining MNCs to empowering women and promoting gender diversity in the international mining industry. It confirms that in a traditionally male-dominated industry such as international mining, management requires extra and specific gender-related expert support to effectively promote women's participation in the workplace.

From work perspectives, results show that mining MNCs can promote women by encouraging them to try new roles and responsibilities. By providing them with skills development, training, resources, support and time, Lao and Thai women like those in this study can progress to various management roles in the organisation. This raises the question of how capacity building for women is constructed and offered to women in the organisation and the community. Mining MNCs may not be able to provide exclusive capacity-building programmes for all women, without engaging women from the beginning of the CSR process. Some strategies include leadership development program for women, introducing flexible work practices, open discussion on career path with all members in the organisation (both men and women), and assertiveness training for men and women in the organisation.

Celebration of femininity is also an important practise to empower women in mining MNCs. The celebration of diversity, not seeing gender difference as weakness, will encourage Lao women to communicate among each other. It will also form a new attitude toward women among men. Participants who work in the mining industry agreed that participating in various social activities such as international women's day, female leadership forum, and gender equality and human rights training can influence their thoughts on doing the right things on behalf of other women in the organisation. They also agreed that working with the management team who address gender issues can positively influence their perceptions towards the company.

Key findings from this study confirm that mining MNCs must understand how to integrate various aspects of diversity (gender, culture, race, ethnicity) and approaches when designing policies and practises to empower women. In sum, this study supports the idea that the participative and empowerment-based method can and will be useful for mining MNCs to empower women in the organisation.

The results of this study carry important implications for stakeholders in international mining industry. Policy makers and practitioners from mining MNCs addressed eclectic approaches that can be implemented to promote women in mining industry. This study highlights different approaches adopted by mining MNCs in order to empower women, and promote gender diversity in the international mining industry. It confirms, in traditionally male-dominant industry such as international mining, management requires extra and specific gender-related expert support in order to effectively promote women's participation in the workplace. Results show that mining MNCs can promote Lao women by encouraging them to try new roles and responsibilities. By providing them skills development, training and time, Lao women can progress to various management roles in the organisation. This raises the question on how capacity building for women is made. Mining MNCs may not be able to provide exclusive capacity building programs for women. Thus, women should be encouraged to actively participate in the existing programs.

Culture is critical in shaping gender roles in any context. It determines how society values the opinions and work of women and men, and it creates not only barriers but also opportunities related to the realisation of women's rights. All cultures change over time—including in response to a variety of external influences—and within a single cultural context there is often a diversity of views about what that culture is or should be. Therefore, companies should understand whose version of 'culture' they are addressing and whose interests are being represented or excluded (Oxfam, 2017).

Future research should investigate proper gender approaches from various stakeholder perspectives. Women in the organisation, clients and suppliers, community and local administrators should be included in order to understand profound local perspectives.

More importantly, it is recommended that future study investigate the Laotian management context that influences actions and policies of mining MNCs. Due to complex sociopolitical factors in the host countries, mining MNCs must be aware of some local constraints that may impede how mining MNCs promote policies on gender equity and women's empowerment.

REFERENCES

Friedman, M. (1962). *Capitalism and freedom*. Chicago: University of Chicago Press.

Grosser, K., & Moon, J. (2005). Gender mainstreaming and corporate social responsibility: Reporting workplace issues. *Journal of Business Ethics*, *62*(4), 327–340. doi:10.100710551-005-5334-3

Kapstein, E. B. (2001). The corporate ethics crucade. *Foreign Affairs*, *80*(5), 105–119. doi:10.2307/20050254

Lahiri-Dutt, K. (2011). Digging women: Towards a new agenda for feminist critiques of mining. *Gender, Place and Culture, 19*(2), 193–212. doi:10.10 80/0966369X.2011.572433

Mercier, L., & Gier, J. (2007). Reconsidering women and gender in mining. *History Compass, 5*(3), 995–1001.

Oxfam. (2017). *Position paper on gender justice and the extractive industries.* Retrieved from https://www.oxfam.org.au/wp-content/uploads/2017/04/ EI_and_GJ_position_paper_v.15_FINAL_03202017_green_Kenny.pdf

Appendix

CASE STUDY: KINGSGATE'S THAI MINE – A LESSON IN FAILED COMMUNITY MANAGEMENT

In mid-January 2017, the Thai government's Department of Primary Industries and Mines ordered the 30-day suspension of activities of Akara Resources, a Thai gold-mining subsidiary of Australia's Kingsgate Consolidated Limited.

The suspension followed a protracted dispute between Akara and local villagers. The locals claimed—and this was voiced predominantly by women—that they had been adversely affected by the mine's activities.

Despite the concerns raised by villagers, Akara continued to issue environmental impact studies that failed to address the concerns.

But when the Thai government assessed the mine's impacts on the environment and health, arsenic and manganese were found to exceed acceptable levels in 282 villagers living near the Kingsgate's Chatree gold mine in Pijit Province.

Kingsgate responded by arguing that 'arsenic and manganese are not used or stored at the Chatree Mining operation now or at any time in its history'. Indeed, it is cyanide rather than arsenic or manganese that is used to leach gold from ore.

Following a public hearing of key community stakeholders in February, the Department of Primary Industries and Mines announced it would lift the suspension order if Akara Resources were to prove its operations do not pose a threat to health. Apparently this did not happen to the government's satisfaction, as an additional 45-day suspension was applied.

A few months later, blood-examination results of villagers residing in an area with a prolonged mining conflict show that hundreds of people have been contaminated with excessive heavy-metallic substances.

Of the children who participated in the examination, 165 had excessive levels of manganese, while the blood of 53 contained excessive levels of arsenic, and 2 indicated excessive levels of syenite.

After the results were revealed in the meeting, Cherdsak Auttaarun, one of the managers of Akara Company, rejected the findings, saying that the examination was not conducted by qualified experts. He added that the findings did not match the information from state agencies, such as the Health Ministry and the Pollution Control Department.

How Could Things Have Gone So Wrong?

The current situation in this mining community offers many lessons for Australian companies investing in developing nations. The systematic lack of engagement of all villagers in Pijit to actively participate in decision-making has led to frustration and dissatisfaction, contributing to the current crisis.

As part of our project funded by the Department of Foreign Affairs and Trade on mining and equitable employment for women in Thailand and Laos, we conducted interviews with 43 locals holding various roles, such as community leaders, workers, protesters, NGOs and farmers in this controversial mining community. Villagers told us of their hopes for improved economic status and a better life.

The legacy of political decentralisation promoted while Thailand was under the rule of the Shinawatra siblings is the expectation that rural communities will be involved in decision-making processes impacting their welfare. At the same time, most villagers we interviewed consider themselves 'uneducated' and 'powerless'.

Akara injects 37 million Thai baht (A$1,465,011) into funds for 27 villages close to the mine. This issue is controversial since the funds are generally placed in the hands of community leaders. Although villagers themselves would dearly like to participate in this decision-making process, in practise most still defer to village heads and local administrators. These funds tend to be tightly controlled by the heads of villages, all male, and those closest to them. Additionally, the company provides disparate financial support to different villages. When resources are accessible, those who have a say in their utilisation are mostly men of relatively high socioeconomic status.

Akara provided villagers a range of social initiatives to help secure goodwill and social licence to operate in the community, including education, microfinance and infrastructure development.

Divergent Agendas

The situation is complex. Demands on the company have arisen from many quarters including government departments, micro-communities from different villages, schools, subcontractors, workers and their family members and even those who have nothing to do with the company. Also, locals are deeply concerned, and in some cases fearful, of the mine's environmental and health impacts, whether related to polluted water, dusty air or noise.

Akara also appears aware and somewhat open to considering the mine-related environmental issues, listing eight challenges in its sustainability report: dust, contaminated water, underground water, water management in the community, noise, carbon dioxide emission, green energy and cyanide management. Regardless, it appears Akara has been unable to find a way to effectively address the community's diverse agenda and concerns about the mine's real and perceived environmental and health impacts.

Resources from the company, whether direct incentives to local government or corporate social responsibility schemes, must create opportunities for the community that will be shared equitably among all stakeholders. More importantly, resources from the company should not create disparity among those of low or high socioeconomic status. The lack of true community consultation that includes members from all walks of life seems to have exacerbated the environmental blame from some community members in Pijit.

Mining by Australian companies can be a development tool in host countries. But the companies involved must be clear about the rationale for the distribution of benefits. Mining companies should facilitate, but not dominate, inclusive decisions by local communities.

Despite the current outcry, all villagers in our study said they want the mine in their community. But they want a trustworthy company that systematically demonstrates strong commitment to environmental protection. Most of all, they want equitable benefit from a mine operating in their backyards, especially since they also suffer its negative consequences.

What Then?

In March 2018, the further investigation was conducted by Naresuan University. The research team's inspection of the first tailing storage facility (TSF1) at Akara Resources' gold mine has confirmed the leakage of contaminated water, while Akara has questioned the reliability of both the report and the researcher (The Nations, 2018). The Thai Department of Special Investigation charged the company on illegitimately acquiring land-rights documents for forestland, of encroaching on a highway and of encroaching on forestland.

Questions

1. If you were the manager working on community-relations issues for this company, what would you do in this case? Please identify stakeholders and steps to be taken.
2. Should the Thai community rely on self-regulated behaviour of this mining company to engage in ethical conduct or on legally binding laws enacted by national government? Discuss, based on this case.
3. Select one international business theory to analyse and explain this situation.

Note

An early version of this case was published in *The Conversation* at https://theconversation.com/kingsgates-thai-mine-a-lesson-in-failed-community-management-37588

Related Readings

To continue IGI Global's long-standing tradition of advancing innovation through emerging research, please find below a compiled list of recommended IGI Global book chapters and journal articles in the areas of gender equality, business ethics, and corporate social responsibility. These related readings will provide additional information and guidance to further enrich your knowledge and assist you with your own research.

Alessandrini, M., & Winter, R. (2015). Systemic Gender Barriers in the Building and Construction Industry: Co-Preneurs as Managers. In S. Moore (Ed.), *Contemporary Global Perspectives on Gender Economics* (pp. 83–100). Hershey, PA: IGI Global. doi:10.4018/978-1-4666-8611-3.ch005

Ang, Y. S. (2015). Ethical Outsourcing and the Act of Acting Together. In R. Wolf, T. Issa, & M. Thiel (Eds.), *Empowering Organizations through Corporate Social Responsibility* (pp. 113–130). Hershey, PA: IGI Global. doi:10.4018/978-1-4666-7294-9.ch006

Avnimelech, G., & Zelekha, Y. (2015). The Impact of Corruption on Entrepreneurship. In R. Wolf & T. Issa (Eds.), *International Business Ethics and Growth Opportunities* (pp. 282–294). Hershey, PA: IGI Global. doi:10.4018/978-1-4666-7419-6.ch013

Ayodele, J. O. (2017). Restorative Justice and Women's Experiences of Violence in Nigeria. In D. Halder & K. Jaishankar (Eds.), *Therapeutic Jurisprudence and Overcoming Violence Against Women* (pp. 44–62). Hershey, PA: IGI Global. doi:10.4018/978-1-5225-2472-4.ch004

Bagdasarov, Z., MacDougall, A. E., Johnson, J. F., & Mumford, M. D. (2015). In Case You Didn't Know: Recommendations for Case-Based Ethics Training. In R. Wolf & T. Issa (Eds.), *International Business Ethics and Growth Opportunities* (pp. 224–249). Hershey, PA: IGI Global. doi:10.4018/978-1-4666-7419-6.ch011

Baraibar-Diez, E., Odriozola, M. D., & Sánchez, J. L. (2017). Storytelling about CSR: Engaging Stakeholders through Storytelling about CSR. In M. Camilleri (Ed.), *CSR 2.0 and the New Era of Corporate Citizenship* (pp. 209–230). Hershey, PA: IGI Global. doi:10.4018/978-1-5225-1842-6.ch011

Barasa, V. N., & Lugo, C. (2015). Is M-PESA a Model for Financial Inclusion and Women Empowerment in Kenya? In S. Moore (Ed.), *Contemporary Global Perspectives on Gender Economics* (pp. 101–123). Hershey, PA: IGI Global. doi:10.4018/978-1-4666-8611-3.ch006

Becchio, G. (2015). A Note on the History of Gender Economics and Feminist Economics: Not the Same Story. In S. Moore (Ed.), *Contemporary Global Perspectives on Gender Economics* (pp. 28–38). Hershey, PA: IGI Global. doi:10.4018/978-1-4666-8611-3.ch002

Begum, R., & Mujtaba, B. G. (2014). Work Ethics Perceptions of Pakistani Employees: Is Work Experience a Factor in Ethical Maturity. *International Journal of Asian Business and Information Management*, 5(1), 1–14. doi:10.4018/ijabim.2014010101

Ben Rejeb, W. (2017). Empirical Evidence on Corporate Governance Impact on CSR Disclosure in Developing Economies: The Tunisian and Egyptian Contexts. In D. Jamali (Ed.), *Comparative Perspectives on Global Corporate Social Responsibility* (pp. 116–137). Hershey, PA: IGI Global. doi:10.4018/978-1-5225-0720-8.ch006

Berberich, R. (2017). Creating Shared Value and Increasing Project Success by Stakeholder Collaboration: A Case in European Manufacturing. In M. Camilleri (Ed.), *CSR 2.0 and the New Era of Corporate Citizenship* (pp. 101–122). Hershey, PA: IGI Global. doi:10.4018/978-1-5225-1842-6.ch006

Berenstok, G., & Saporta, I. (2015). The Moral Limitations of the Rational-Monistic Model: A Revision of the Concept of Rationality and Rational Action. In R. Wolf & T. Issa (Eds.), *International Business Ethics and Growth Opportunities* (pp. 127–145). Hershey, PA: IGI Global. doi:10.4018/978-1-4666-7419-6.ch006

Camilleri, M. A. (2017). The Corporate Sustainability and Responsibility Proposition: A Review and Appraisal. In M. Camilleri (Ed.), *CSR 2.0 and the New Era of Corporate Citizenship* (pp. 1–16). Hershey, PA: IGI Global. doi:10.4018/978-1-5225-1842-6.ch001

Chandra, R. R., & Jaishankar, K. (2017). Female Victims of Labor Exploitation Vis-à-Vis Labor Courts in the Southern Tamil Nadu, India: Therapeutic Jurisprudence Solutions for the Prevention of Secondary Victimization. In D. Halder & K. Jaishankar (Eds.), *Therapeutic Jurisprudence and Overcoming Violence Against Women* (pp. 171–181). Hershey, PA: IGI Global. doi:10.4018/978-1-5225-2472-4.ch011

Chowdhury, F. (2016). Permanently Temporary: The Production of Race, Class, and Gender Hierarchies through a Study of Canada's Temporary Foreign Worker Program. In N. Mahtab, S. Parker, F. Kabir, T. Haque, A. Sabur, & A. Sowad (Eds.), *Discourse Analysis as a Tool for Understanding Gender Identity, Representation, and Equality* (pp. 175–203). Hershey, PA: IGI Global. doi:10.4018/978-1-5225-0225-8.ch009

Chowdhury, F. (2016). Permanently Temporary: The Production of Race, Class, and Gender Hierarchies through a Study of Canada's Temporary Foreign Worker Program. In N. Mahtab, S. Parker, F. Kabir, T. Haque, A. Sabur, & A. Sowad (Eds.), *Discourse Analysis as a Tool for Understanding Gender Identity, Representation, and Equality* (pp. 175–203). Hershey, PA: IGI Global. doi:10.4018/978-1-5225-0225-8.ch009

Churchill, S. K. (2015). Impact of Microfinance on Female Empowerment: A Review of the Empirical Literature. In S. Moore (Ed.), *Contemporary Global Perspectives on Gender Economics* (pp. 39–54). Hershey, PA: IGI Global. doi:10.4018/978-1-4666-8611-3.ch003

Ciani, A., Diotallevi, F., Rocchi, L., Grigore, A. M., Coduti, C., & Belgrado, E. (2015). Corporate Social Responsibility (CSR): Theory, Regulations, and New Paradigms in the Framework of Sustainable Development Strategy. In R. Wolf, T. Issa, & M. Thiel (Eds.), *Empowering Organizations through Corporate Social Responsibility* (pp. 166–190). Hershey, PA: IGI Global. doi:10.4018/978-1-4666-7294-9.ch009

Ciani, A., Rocchi, L., Paolotti, L., Diotallevi, F., Guerra, J. B., Fernandez, F., ... Grigore, A. (2015). Corporate Social Responsibility (CSR): A Cross-Cultural Comparison of Practices. In R. Wolf, T. Issa, & M. Thiel (Eds.), *Empowering Organizations through Corporate Social Responsibility* (pp. 73–96). Hershey, PA: IGI Global. doi:10.4018/978-1-4666-7294-9.ch004

Clayton, T., & West, N. (2015). In Search of the Good Dam: A Role for Corporate Social Responsibility in Mekong Hydropower Development. In R. Wolf, T. Issa, & M. Thiel (Eds.), *Empowering Organizations through Corporate Social Responsibility* (pp. 288–306). Hershey, PA: IGI Global. doi:10.4018/978-1-4666-7294-9.ch015

Coleman, A. R. (2016). Blogging Their Way Out of Disadvantage: Women, Identity and Agency in the Blogosphere. In R. English & R. Johns (Eds.), *Gender Considerations in Online Consumption Behavior and Internet Use* (pp. 64–80). Hershey, PA: IGI Global. doi:10.4018/978-1-5225-0010-0.ch005

Corazza, L. (2017). The Standardization of Down-Streamed Small Business Social Responsibility (SBSR): SMEs and Their Sustainability Reporting Practices. *Information Resources Management Journal*, *30*(4), 39–52. doi:10.4018/IRMJ.2017100103

Cramm, D., & Erwee, R. (2015). Business Ethics Competencies: Controversies, Contexts, and Implications for Business Ethics Training. In R. Wolf & T. Issa (Eds.), *International Business Ethics and Growth Opportunities* (pp. 201–223). Hershey, PA: IGI Global. doi:10.4018/978-1-4666-7419-6.ch010

Crewe, H. (2017). Can Therapeutic Jurisprudence Improve the Rights of Female Prisoners? In D. Halder & K. Jaishankar (Eds.), *Therapeutic Jurisprudence and Overcoming Violence Against Women* (pp. 248–263). Hershey, PA: IGI Global. doi:10.4018/978-1-5225-2472-4.ch015

Dale, N. F. (2016). Gender and Other Factors That Influence Tourism Preferences. In R. English & R. Johns (Eds.), *Gender Considerations in Online Consumption Behavior and Internet Use* (pp. 13–31). Hershey, PA: IGI Global. doi:10.4018/978-1-5225-0010-0.ch002

Davidson, D. K., & Yin, J. (2017). Corporate Social Responsibility (CSR) in China: A Contextual Exploration. In D. Jamali (Ed.), *Comparative Perspectives on Global Corporate Social Responsibility* (pp. 28–48). Hershey, PA: IGI Global. doi:10.4018/978-1-5225-0720-8.ch002 de Burgh-Woodman, H., Bressan, A., & Torrisi, A. (2017). An Evaluation of the State of the CSR Field in Australia: Perspectives from the Banking and Mining Sectors. In D. Jamali (Ed.), *Comparative Perspectives on Global Corporate Social Responsibility* (pp. 138–164). Hershey, PA: IGI Global. doi:10.4018/978-1-5225-0720-8.ch007

de Burgh-Woodman, H., Saha, A., Somasundram, K., & Torrisi, A. (2015). Sowing the Seeds for Ethical Business Leadership through Business Education. In R. Wolf & T. Issa (Eds.), *International Business Ethics and Growth Opportunities* (pp. 177–200). Hershey, PA: IGI Global. doi:10.4018/978-1-4666-7419-6.ch009

Del Chiappa, G., Pinna, M., & Atzeni, M. (2017). Barriers to Responsible Tourist Behaviour: A Cluster Analysis in the Context of Italy. In M. Camilleri (Ed.), *CSR 2.0 and the New Era of Corporate Citizenship* (pp. 290–308). Hershey, PA: IGI Global. doi:10.4018/978-1-5225-1842-6.ch015

Denner, J., Ortiz, E., & Werner, L. (2014). Women and Men in Computer Science: The Role of Gaming in their Educational Goals. In J. Prescott & J. McGurren (Eds.), *Gender Considerations and Influence in the Digital Media and Gaming Industry* (pp. 18–35). Hershey, PA: IGI Global. doi:10.4018/978-1-4666-6142-4.ch002

Devereux, M. T., & Gallarza, M. G. (2017). Social Value Co-Creation: Insights from Consumers, Employees, and Managers. In M. Camilleri (Ed.), *CSR 2.0 and the New Era of Corporate Citizenship* (pp. 76–100). Hershey, PA: IGI Global. doi:10.4018/978-1-5225-1842-6.ch005

Dikeç, A., Kane, V., & Çapar, N. (2017). Cross-Country and Cross-Sector CSR Variations: A Comparative Analysis of CSR Reporting in the U.S., South Korea, and Turkey. In D. Jamali (Ed.), *Comparative Perspectives on Global Corporate Social Responsibility* (pp. 69–95). Hershey, PA: IGI Global. doi:10.4018/978-1-5225-0720-8.ch004

Dörries, A. (2015). A Matter of Justice: Building Trust among Hospital Managers and Physicians. In R. Wolf & T. Issa (Eds.), *International Business Ethics and Growth Opportunities* (pp. 24–41). Hershey, PA: IGI Global. doi:10.4018/978-1-4666-7419-6.ch002

Dutt, S. C. (2015). Money of Her Own and the Politics of Women's Empowerment. In S. Moore (Ed.), *Contemporary Global Perspectives on Gender Economics* (pp. 55–81). Hershey, PA: IGI Global. doi:10.4018/978-1-4666-8611-3.ch004

El Sherif, S. (2017). Violence Against Women and Therapeutic Jurisprudence in Egypt: An Islamic Approach. In D. Halder & K. Jaishankar (Eds.), *Therapeutic Jurisprudence and Overcoming Violence Against Women* (pp. 15–29). Hershey, PA: IGI Global. doi:10.4018/978-1-5225-2472-4.ch002

Elicegui-Reyes, J. I., Barrena-Martínez, J., & Romero-Fernández, P. M. (2017). Emotional Capital and Sustainability in Family Businesses: Human Resource Management Perspective and Sustainability. In M. Camilleri (Ed.), *CSR 2.0 and the New Era of Corporate Citizenship* (pp. 231–250). Hershey, PA: IGI Global. doi:10.4018/978-1-5225-1842-6.ch012

Elliott, L., & Prescott, J. (2014). The Only Girl in the Class!: Female Students' Experiences of Gaming Courses and Views of the Industry. In J. Prescott & J. McGurren (Eds.), *Gender Considerations and Influence in the Digital Media and Gaming Industry* (pp. 36–55). Hershey, PA: IGI Global. doi:10.4018/978-1-4666-6142-4.ch003

English, R. (2016). Techno Teacher Moms: Web 2.0 Connecting Mothers in the Home Education Community. In R. English & R. Johns (Eds.), *Gender Considerations in Online Consumption Behavior and Internet Use* (pp. 96–111). Hershey, PA: IGI Global. doi:10.4018/978-1-5225-0010-0.ch007

English, R., & Nykvist, S. (2016). Looking At the Other Side: Families, Public Health and Anti-Vaccination. In R. English & R. Johns (Eds.), *Gender Considerations in Online Consumption Behavior and Internet Use* (pp. 150–160). Hershey, PA: IGI Global. doi:10.4018/978-1-5225-0010-0.ch010

Ferdowsi, L. (2016). Intersections of Gender, Sex, and Power: Control over Women's Bodies and Sexuality Amongst the Bangladeshi Diaspora in Britain. In N. Mahtab, S. Parker, F. Kabir, T. Haque, A. Sabur, & A. Sowad (Eds.), *Discourse Analysis as a Tool for Understanding Gender Identity, Representation, and Equality* (pp. 1–24). Hershey, PA: IGI Global. doi:10.4018/978-1-5225-0225-8.ch001

Ferdowsi, L. (2016). Intersections of Gender, Sex, and Power: Control over Women's Bodies and Sexuality Amongst the Bangladeshi Diaspora in Britain. In N. Mahtab, S. Parker, F. Kabir, T. Haque, A. Sabur, & A. Sowad (Eds.), *Discourse Analysis as a Tool for Understanding Gender Identity, Representation, and Equality* (pp. 1–24). Hershey, PA: IGI Global. doi:10.4018/978-1-5225-0225-8.ch001

Fisherman, S. (2016). Body Image and Wellbeing in Religious Male and Female Youth in Israel: An Educational Challenge. In B. Glimps & T. Ford (Eds.), *Gender and Diversity Issues in Religious-Based Institutions and Organizations* (pp. 51–79). Hershey, PA: IGI Global. doi:10.4018/978-1-4666-8772-1.ch003

Ford, C. P. (2015). New Kids on the Block: What Gender Economics and Palermo Tell Us about Trafficking in Human Beings. In S. Moore (Ed.), *Contemporary Global Perspectives on Gender Economics* (pp. 167–186). Hershey, PA: IGI Global. doi:10.4018/978-1-4666-8611-3.ch009

Fujihara, M. (2014). Career Development among Japanese Female Game Developers: Perspective from Life Stories of Creative Professionals. In J. Prescott & J. McGurren (Eds.), *Gender Considerations and Influence in the Digital Media and Gaming Industry* (pp. 110–124). Hershey, PA: IGI Global. doi:10.4018/978-1-4666-6142-4.ch006

García de Leaniz, P. M., & Gómez-López, R. (2017). Responsible Management in the CSR 2.0 Era. In M. Camilleri (Ed.), *CSR 2.0 and the New Era of Corporate Citizenship* (pp. 37–54). Hershey, PA: IGI Global. doi:10.4018/978-1-5225-1842-6.ch003

Gavrielides, T. (2017). Reconciling Restorative Justice with the Law for Violence Against Women in Europe: A Scheme of Structured and Unstructured Models. In D. Halder & K. Jaishankar (Eds.), *Therapeutic Jurisprudence and Overcoming Violence Against Women* (pp. 106–120). Hershey, PA: IGI Global. doi:10.4018/978-1-5225-2472-4.ch007

Geneve, A. (2014). Women's Participation in the Australian Digital Content Industry. In J. Prescott & J. McGurren (Eds.), *Gender Considerations and Influence in the Digital Media and Gaming Industry* (pp. 125–142). Hershey, PA: IGI Global. doi:10.4018/978-1-4666-6142-4.ch007

Grant, C. T., & Grant, K. A. (2016). Improving Moral Behaviour in the Business Use of ICT: The Potential of Positive Psychology. *International Journal of Cyber Ethics in Education, 4*(2), 1–21. doi:10.4018/IJCEE.2016070101

Griffith, J. A., Zeni, T. A., & Johnson, G. (2015). Utilizing Emotions for Ethical Decision Making in Leadership. In R. Wolf & T. Issa (Eds.), *International Business Ethics and Growth Opportunities* (pp. 158–175). Hershey, PA: IGI Global. doi:10.4018/978-1-4666-7419-6.ch008

Growe, R., & Person, W. A. (2017). Toxic Workplace Environment and Its Impact on Women Professors in the United States: The Imperative Need for Therapeutic Jurisprudence Practices in Higher Education. In D. Halder & K. Jaishankar (Eds.), *Therapeutic Jurisprudence and Overcoming Violence Against Women* (pp. 182–197). Hershey, PA: IGI Global. doi:10.4018/978-1-5225-2472-4.ch012

Gul, M. C., & Kaytaz, M. (2017). CSR and Social Marketing as Enablers of Recovery after the Global Recession: The Turkish Banking Industry. In M. Camilleri (Ed.), *CSR 2.0 and the New Era of Corporate Citizenship* (pp. 274–289). Hershey, PA: IGI Global. doi:10.4018/978-1-5225-1842-6.ch014

Hack-Polay, D., & Qiu, H. (2017). Doing Good Doing Well: Discussion of CSR in the Pulp and Paper Industry in the Asian Context. In D. Jamali (Ed.), *Comparative Perspectives on Global Corporate Social Responsibility* (pp. 226–240). Hershey, PA: IGI Global. doi:10.4018/978-1-5225-0720-8.ch011

Halder, D. (2017). Revenge Porn Against Women and the Applicability of Therapeutic Jurisprudence: A Comparative Analysis of Regulations in India, Pakistan, and Bangladesh. In D. Halder & K. Jaishankar (Eds.), *Therapeutic Jurisprudence and Overcoming Violence Against Women* (pp. 282–292). Hershey, PA: IGI Global. doi:10.4018/978-1-5225-2472-4.ch017

Halder, D., & Jaishankar, K. (2017). Love Marriages, Inter-Caste Violence, and Therapeutic Jurisprudential Approach of the Courts in India. In D. Halder & K. Jaishankar (Eds.), *Therapeutic Jurisprudence and Overcoming Violence Against Women* (pp. 30–42). Hershey, PA: IGI Global. doi:10.4018/978-1-5225-2472-4.ch003

Haro-de-Rosario, A., del Mar Gálvez-Rodríguez, M., & Caba-Pérez, M. D. (2017). Determinants of Corporate Social Responsibility Disclosure in Latin American Companies: An Analysis of the Oil and Gas Sector. In D. Jamali (Ed.), *Comparative Perspectives on Global Corporate Social Responsibility* (pp. 165–184). Hershey, PA: IGI Global. doi:10.4018/978-1-5225-0720-8.ch008

Harris-Smith, Y. J. (2016). Spiritual Health Identity: Placing Black Women's Lives in the Center of Analysis. In B. Glimps & T. Ford (Eds.), *Gender and Diversity Issues in Religious-Based Institutions and Organizations* (pp. 1–23). Hershey, PA: IGI Global. doi:10.4018/978-1-4666-8772-1.ch001

Hassan, A., & Lund-Thomsen, P. (2017). Multi-Stakeholder Initiatives and Corporate Social Responsibility in Global Value Chains: Towards an Analytical Framework and a Methodology. In D. Jamali (Ed.), *Comparative Perspectives on Global Corporate Social Responsibility* (pp. 241–257). Hershey, PA: IGI Global. doi:10.4018/978-1-5225-0720-8.ch012

Herzog-Evans, M. (2017). Violence Against Women Programmes in a North-Eastern French City: Issues of Safety, Collaboration, Gender, "McJustice," and Evidence-Based Practices. In D. Halder & K. Jaishankar (Eds.), *Therapeutic Jurisprudence and Overcoming Violence Against Women* (pp. 85–105). Hershey, PA: IGI Global. doi:10.4018/978-1-5225-2472-4.ch006

Higgs, E. T. (2016). Becoming 'Multi-Racial': The Young Women's Christian Association in Kenya, 1955-1965. In B. Glimps & T. Ford (Eds.), *Gender and Diversity Issues in Religious-Based Institutions and Organizations* (pp. 24–50). Hershey, PA: IGI Global. doi:10.4018/978-1-4666-8772-1.ch002

Holland, P. G., & Alakavuklar, O. N. (2017). Corporate Social Responsibility (CSR) Reporting and Seeking Legitimacy of Māori Communities: A Case from Aotearoa New Zealand Energy Sector. In M. Camilleri (Ed.), *CSR 2.0 and the New Era of Corporate Citizenship* (pp. 123–146). Hershey, PA: IGI Global. doi:10.4018/978-1-5225-1842-6.ch007

Hyatt, K. (2016). Effectiveness and Content of Corporate Codes of Ethics as a Model for University Honor Codes. *International Journal of Technology and Educational Marketing*, *6*(1), 52–69. doi:10.4018/IJTEM.2016010104

Idris, S. (2015). Economic Empowerment of Women in Pakistan. In S. Moore (Ed.), *Contemporary Global Perspectives on Gender Economics* (pp. 124–145). Hershey, PA: IGI Global. doi:10.4018/978-1-4666-8611-3.ch007

Islam, A. (2016). Disparity between Boys and Girls: Concerning Sports in Secondary Level Academic Institutions. In N. Mahtab, S. Parker, F. Kabir, T. Haque, A. Sabur, & A. Sowad (Eds.), *Discourse Analysis as a Tool for Understanding Gender Identity, Representation, and Equality* (pp. 157–174). Hershey, PA: IGI Global. doi:10.4018/978-1-5225-0225-8.ch008

Islam, A. (2016). Disparity between Boys and Girls: Concerning Sports in Secondary Level Academic Institutions. In N. Mahtab, S. Parker, F. Kabir, T. Haque, A. Sabur, & A. Sowad (Eds.), *Discourse Analysis as a Tool for Understanding Gender Identity, Representation, and Equality* (pp. 157–174). Hershey, PA: IGI Global. doi:10.4018/978-1-5225-0225-8.ch008

Issa, T., & Pick, D. (2017). Teaching Business Ethics Post GFC: A Corporate Social Responsibility of Universities. In D. Jamali (Ed.), *Comparative Perspectives on Global Corporate Social Responsibility* (pp. 290–307). Hershey, PA: IGI Global. doi:10.4018/978-1-5225-0720-8.ch015

Jabin, M. (2016). Struggle against ICT-Based Violence: Locating Socialization Process of Young Men as a Hidden Cause of Women's Vulnerability. In N. Mahtab, S. Parker, F. Kabir, T. Haque, A. Sabur, & A. Sowad (Eds.), *Discourse Analysis as a Tool for Understanding Gender Identity, Representation, and Equality* (pp. 218–235). Hershey, PA: IGI Global. doi:10.4018/978-1-5225-0225-8.ch011

Jabin, M. (2016). Struggle against ICT-Based Violence: Locating Socialization Process of Young Men as a Hidden Cause of Women's Vulnerability. In N. Mahtab, S. Parker, F. Kabir, T. Haque, A. Sabur, & A. Sowad (Eds.), *Discourse Analysis as a Tool for Understanding Gender Identity, Representation, and Equality* (pp. 218–235). Hershey, PA: IGI Global. doi:10.4018/978-1-5225-0225-8.ch011

Jackson, K. A. (2016). How Movember's Online Community Influences Australia's Men's Health Debate. In R. English & R. Johns (Eds.), *Gender Considerations in Online Consumption Behavior and Internet Use* (pp. 125–149). Hershey, PA: IGI Global. doi:10.4018/978-1-5225-0010-0.ch009

Jahan, F. R. (2016). Agency, Gender Identities, and Clothing Consumption: The Discourse on Garment Workers. In N. Mahtab, S. Parker, F. Kabir, T. Haque, A. Sabur, & A. Sowad (Eds.), *Discourse Analysis as a Tool for Understanding Gender Identity, Representation, and Equality* (pp. 136–156). Hershey, PA: IGI Global. doi:10.4018/978-1-5225-0225-8.ch007

Jamali, D., Abdallah, H., & Matar, F. (2016). Opportunities and Challenges for CSR Mainstreaming in Business Schools. *International Journal of Technology and Educational Marketing*, 6(2), 1–29. doi:10.4018/IJTEM.2016070101

James, H. S. Jr. (2015). Why Do Good People Do Bad Things in Business?: Lessons from Research for Responsible Business Managers. In R. Wolf & T. Issa (Eds.), *International Business Ethics and Growth Opportunities* (pp. 1–23). Hershey, PA: IGI Global. doi:10.4018/978-1-4666-7419-6.ch001

Johns, R. (2016). Increasing Value of a Tangible Product through Intangible Attributes: Value Co-Creation and Brand Building within Online Communities – Virtual Communities and Value. In R. English & R. Johns (Eds.), *Gender Considerations in Online Consumption Behavior and Internet Use* (pp. 112–124). Hershey, PA: IGI Global. doi:10.4018/978-1-5225-0010-0.ch008

Johns, R., Mackrell, D., Dale, N. F., & Dewan, S. (2016). The Online Feminine Mystique: Developing a Research Agenda for Women's Use of Social Media. In R. English & R. Johns (Eds.), *Gender Considerations in Online Consumption Behavior and Internet Use* (pp. 1–12). Hershey, PA: IGI Global. doi:10.4018/978-1-5225-0010-0.ch001

Kaplan, J., & Montiel, I. (2017). East vs. West Approaches to Reporting Corporate Sustainability Strategies to the World: Corporate Sustainability Reporting: East vs. West. In D. Jamali (Ed.), *Comparative Perspectives on Global Corporate Social Responsibility* (pp. 49–68). Hershey, PA: IGI Global. doi:10.4018/978-1-5225-0720-8.ch003

Kaufmann, G. (2015). Analyzing CSR's Expectation Gap through the World System Differential. In R. Wolf, T. Issa, & M. Thiel (Eds.), *Empowering Organizations through Corporate Social Responsibility* (pp. 209–239). Hershey, PA: IGI Global. doi:10.4018/978-1-4666-7294-9.ch011

Kay, M. J. (2015). Corporate Sustainability Programs and Reporting: Responsibility Commitment and Thought Leadership at Starbucks. In R. Wolf, T. Issa, & M. Thiel (Eds.), *Empowering Organizations through Corporate Social Responsibility* (pp. 307–323). Hershey, PA: IGI Global. doi:10.4018/978-1-4666-7294-9.ch016

Kelly, M., & Jetnikoff, A. (2016). It's My Site, and I'll Do What I Want: Performing Female Identity through Digital Identity Curation in Online Spaces. In R. English & R. Johns (Eds.), *Gender Considerations in Online Consumption Behavior and Internet Use* (pp. 50–63). Hershey, PA: IGI Global. doi:10.4018/978-1-5225-0010-0.ch004

Khan, M. (2016). Implications of Citizenship Discourse on Female Labour Force Participation: A Case Study of Bangladeshi Women in the UK. In N. Mahtab, S. Parker, F. Kabir, T. Haque, A. Sabur, & A. Sowad (Eds.), *Discourse Analysis as a Tool for Understanding Gender Identity, Representation, and Equality* (pp. 25–49). Hershey, PA: IGI Global. doi:10.4018/978-1-5225-0225-8.ch002

Khan, M. (2016). Implications of Citizenship Discourse on Female Labour Force Participation: A Case Study of Bangladeshi Women in the UK. In N. Mahtab, S. Parker, F. Kabir, T. Haque, A. Sabur, & A. Sowad (Eds.), *Discourse Analysis as a Tool for Understanding Gender Identity, Representation, and Equality* (pp. 25–49). Hershey, PA: IGI Global. doi:10.4018/978-1-5225-0225-8.ch002

Khanum, R. A. (2016). Equality and Differences: Some Feminist Thoughts. In N. Mahtab, S. Parker, F. Kabir, T. Haque, A. Sabur, & A. Sowad (Eds.), *Discourse Analysis as a Tool for Understanding Gender Identity, Representation, and Equality* (pp. 204–217). Hershey, PA: IGI Global. doi:10.4018/978-1-5225-0225-8.ch010

Khanum, R. A. (2016). Equality and Differences: Some Feminist Thoughts. In N. Mahtab, S. Parker, F. Kabir, T. Haque, A. Sabur, & A. Sowad (Eds.), *Discourse Analysis as a Tool for Understanding Gender Identity, Representation, and Equality* (pp. 204–217). Hershey, PA: IGI Global. doi:10.4018/978-1-5225-0225-8.ch010

King, A. E., & Douai, A. (2014). From the "Damsel in Distress" to Girls' Games and Beyond: Gender and Children's Gaming. In J. Prescott & J. McGurren (Eds.), *Gender Considerations and Influence in the Digital Media and Gaming Industry* (pp. 1–17). Hershey, PA: IGI Global. doi:10.4018/978-1-4666-6142-4.ch001

Koriat, N., & Gelbard, R. (2015). Insourcing of IT Workers: A Win-Win Strategy - Economic Analysis of IT Units in Israeli Governmental Offices. In R. Wolf, T. Issa, & M. Thiel (Eds.), *Empowering Organizations through Corporate Social Responsibility* (pp. 241–254). Hershey, PA: IGI Global. doi:10.4018/978-1-4666-7294-9.ch012

Kousar, H. (2017). Sexual Violence in the University Campuses of Delhi, India, and Therapeutic Jurisprudence for Justice to Victims: A Qualitative Study. In D. Halder & K. Jaishankar (Eds.), *Therapeutic Jurisprudence and Overcoming Violence Against Women* (pp. 198–212). Hershey, PA: IGI Global. doi:10.4018/978-1-5225-2472-4.ch013

Kujala, J. (2015). Branding as a Tool for CSR. In R. Wolf, T. Issa, & M. Thiel (Eds.), *Empowering Organizations through Corporate Social Responsibility* (pp. 266–287). Hershey, PA: IGI Global. doi:10.4018/978-1-4666-7294-9.ch014

Lanzerath, D. (2015). Ethics in Business and Human Flourishing: Integrating Economy in Life. In R. Wolf & T. Issa (Eds.), *International Business Ethics and Growth Opportunities* (pp. 74–96). Hershey, PA: IGI Global. doi:10.4018/978-1-4666-7419-6.ch004

Loverock, D. T., Kool, R., & Kajzer-Mitchell, I. (2015). Workplace Culture as a Driver for Social Change: Influencing Employee Pro-Environmental Behaviors. In R. Wolf, T. Issa, & M. Thiel (Eds.), *Empowering Organizations through Corporate Social Responsibility* (pp. 29–50). Hershey, PA: IGI Global. doi:10.4018/978-1-4666-7294-9.ch002

Makaros, A. (2015). Corporate Social Responsibility: Practice Models for Building Business-Community Collaborations. In R. Wolf, T. Issa, & M. Thiel (Eds.), *Empowering Organizations through Corporate Social Responsibility* (pp. 191–208). Hershey, PA: IGI Global. doi:10.4018/978-1-4666-7294-9.ch010

Manroop, L., & Harrison, J. (2015). The Ethics Portfolio: Building and Promoting Ethical Culture in an Organization. In R. Wolf & T. Issa (Eds.), *International Business Ethics and Growth Opportunities* (pp. 97–126). Hershey, PA: IGI Global. doi:10.4018/978-1-4666-7419-6.ch005

Margetts, T., & Holland, E. (2015). The Case for Group Heterogeneity. In S. Moore (Ed.), *Contemporary Global Perspectives on Gender Economics* (pp. 146–165). Hershey, PA: IGI Global. doi:10.4018/978-1-4666-8611-3.ch008

McGill, M. M., Decker, A., & Settle, A. (2014). A Framework for Addressing Gender Imbalance in the Game Industry through Outreach. In J. Prescott & J. McGurren (Eds.), *Gender Considerations and Influence in the Digital Media and Gaming Industry* (pp. 186–205). Hershey, PA: IGI Global. doi:10.4018/978-1-4666-6142-4.ch010

Moore, S. (2015). Gender Economics: An Introduction to Contemporary Gender Economics. In S. Moore (Ed.), *Contemporary Global Perspectives on Gender Economics* (pp. 1–26). Hershey, PA: IGI Global. doi:10.4018/978-1-4666-8611-3.ch001

Nedelko, Z., & Potocan, V. (2015). Perception of Corporate Social Responsibility by the Employees: Evidence from Slovenia. In R. Wolf, T. Issa, & M. Thiel (Eds.), *Empowering Organizations through Corporate Social Responsibility* (pp. 51–72). Hershey, PA: IGI Global. doi:10.4018/978-1-4666-7294-9.ch003

Nguyen, L. D., Lee, K., Mujtaba, B. G., & Silanont, S. P. (2014). Business Ethics Perceptions of Working Adults: A Study in Thailand. *International Journal of Asian Business and Information Management, 5*(2), 23–40. doi:10.4018/ijabim.2014040103

Noguti, V., Singh, S., & Waller, D. S. (2016). Gender Differences in Motivations to Use Social Networking Sites. In R. English & R. Johns (Eds.), *Gender Considerations in Online Consumption Behavior and Internet Use* (pp. 32–49). Hershey, PA: IGI Global. doi:10.4018/978-1-5225-0010-0.ch003

Okoń-Horodyńska, E. (2015). Innovation, Innovativeness, and Gender: Approaching Innovative Gender. In S. Moore (Ed.), *Contemporary Global Perspectives on Gender Economics* (pp. 244–263). Hershey, PA: IGI Global. doi:10.4018/978-1-4666-8611-3.ch013

Olukolu, Y. R. (2017). Harmful Traditional Practices, Laws, and Reproductive Rights of Women in Nigeria: A Therapeutic Jurisprudence Approach. In D. Halder & K. Jaishankar (Eds.), *Therapeutic Jurisprudence and Overcoming Violence Against Women* (pp. 1–14). Hershey, PA: IGI Global. doi:10.4018/978-1-5225-2472-4.ch001

Osman, M. N. (2017). Internet-Based Social Reporting in Emerging Economies: Insights from Public Banks in Egypt and the UAE. In D. Jamali (Ed.), *Comparative Perspectives on Global Corporate Social Responsibility* (pp. 96–115). Hershey, PA: IGI Global. doi:10.4018/978-1-5225-0720-8.ch005

Parsa, F. (2016). Challenges of Iranian Women to Change the Gender Discriminatory Law. In N. Mahtab, S. Parker, F. Kabir, T. Haque, A. Sabur, & A. Sowad (Eds.), *Discourse Analysis as a Tool for Understanding Gender Identity, Representation, and Equality* (pp. 74–89). Hershey, PA: IGI Global. doi:10.4018/978-1-5225-0225-8.ch004

Parsa, F. (2016). Challenges of Iranian Women to Change the Gender Discriminatory Law. In N. Mahtab, S. Parker, F. Kabir, T. Haque, A. Sabur, & A. Sowad (Eds.), *Discourse Analysis as a Tool for Understanding Gender Identity, Representation, and Equality* (pp. 74–89). Hershey, PA: IGI Global. doi:10.4018/978-1-5225-0225-8.ch004

Pascal, A. (2015). Business Ethics is Socio-Political, or Not at All: The Case of Roşia Montana. In R. Wolf & T. Issa (Eds.), *International Business Ethics and Growth Opportunities* (pp. 251–281). Hershey, PA: IGI Global. doi:10.4018/978-1-4666-7419-6.ch012

Peacock, J. S., & Chowdhury, S. A. (2016). The Effect of Colonialism on the Bangladeshi Female Immigrant in Britain. In N. Mahtab, S. Parker, F. Kabir, T. Haque, A. Sabur, & A. Sowad (Eds.), *Discourse Analysis as a Tool for Understanding Gender Identity, Representation, and Equality* (pp. 90–98). Hershey, PA: IGI Global. doi:10.4018/978-1-5225-0225-8.ch005

Peacock, J. S., & Chowdhury, S. A. (2016). The Effect of Colonialism on the Bangladeshi Female Immigrant in Britain. In N. Mahtab, S. Parker, F. Kabir, T. Haque, A. Sabur, & A. Sowad (Eds.), *Discourse Analysis as a Tool for Understanding Gender Identity, Representation, and Equality* (pp. 90–98). Hershey, PA: IGI Global. doi:10.4018/978-1-5225-0225-8.ch005

Pittaro, M. (2017). Pornography and Global Sex Trafficking: A Proposal for Therapeutic Jurisprudence as Court Innovation in the United States. In D. Halder & K. Jaishankar (Eds.), *Therapeutic Jurisprudence and Overcoming Violence Against Women* (pp. 121–133). Hershey, PA: IGI Global. doi:10.4018/978-1-5225-2472-4.ch008

Prescott, J., & Bogg, J. (2014). Female Game Workers: Career Development, and Aspirations. In J. Prescott & J. McGurren (Eds.), *Gender Considerations and Influence in the Digital Media and Gaming Industry* (pp. 206–222). Hershey, PA: IGI Global. doi:10.4018/978-1-4666-6142-4.ch011

Prescott, J., & Bogg, J. (2014). *Gender Divide and the Computer Game Industry* (pp. 1–321). Hershey, PA: IGI Global. doi:10.4018/978-1-4666-4534-9

Prescott, J., & Bogg, J. (2014). The Experiences of Women Working in the Computer Games Industry: An In-Depth Qualitative Study. In J. Prescott & J. McGurren (Eds.), *Gender Considerations and Influence in the Digital Media and Gaming Industry* (pp. 92–109). Hershey, PA: IGI Global. doi:10.4018/978-1-4666-6142-4.ch005

Priyadarshini, D. (2017). Women and the Impact of the Shifting Jurisprudence in New Delhi, India: How Therapeutic for Urban Slum-Dwellers? In D. Halder & K. Jaishankar (Eds.), *Therapeutic Jurisprudence and Overcoming Violence Against Women* (pp. 264–281). Hershey, PA: IGI Global. doi:10.4018/978-1-5225-2472-4.ch016

Puaschunder, J. (2017). The Call for Global Responsible Inter-Generational Leadership: The Quest of an Integration of Inter-Generational Equity in Corporate Social Responsibility (CSR) Models. In D. Jamali (Ed.), *Comparative Perspectives on Global Corporate Social Responsibility* (pp. 276–289). Hershey, PA: IGI Global. doi:10.4018/978-1-5225-0720-8.ch014

Pugh, V. M. (2014). A Look inside the Current Climate of the Video Game Industry. In J. Prescott & J. McGurren (Eds.), *Gender Considerations and Influence in the Digital Media and Gaming Industry* (pp. 82–91). Hershey, PA: IGI Global. doi:10.4018/978-1-4666-6142-4.ch004

Pugh, V. M. (2014). Lessons from the STEM Sector. In J. Prescott & J. McGurren (Eds.), *Gender Considerations and Influence in the Digital Media and Gaming Industry* (pp. 175–185). Hershey, PA: IGI Global. doi:10.4018/978-1-4666-6142-4.ch009

Radovic, V. M. (2017). Corporate Sustainability and Responsibility and Disaster Risk Reduction: A Serbian Overview. In M. Camilleri (Ed.), *CSR 2.0 and the New Era of Corporate Citizenship* (pp. 147–164). Hershey, PA: IGI Global. doi:10.4018/978-1-5225-1842-6.ch008

Rahdari, A. H. (2017). Fostering Responsible Business: Evidence from Leading Corporate Social Responsibility and Sustainability Networks. In M. Camilleri (Ed.), *CSR 2.0 and the New Era of Corporate Citizenship* (pp. 309–330). Hershey, PA: IGI Global. doi:10.4018/978-1-5225-1842-6.ch016

Raimi, L. (2017). Leveraging CSR as a 'support-aid' for Triple Bottom-Line Development in Nigeria: Evidence from the Telecommunication Industry. In D. Jamali (Ed.), *Comparative Perspectives on Global Corporate Social Responsibility* (pp. 208–225). Hershey, PA: IGI Global. doi:10.4018/978-1-5225-0720-8.ch010

Reeves, M. (2016). Social Media: It Can Play a Positive Role in Education. In R. English & R. Johns (Eds.), *Gender Considerations in Online Consumption Behavior and Internet Use* (pp. 82–95). Hershey, PA: IGI Global. doi:10.4018/978-1-5225-0010-0.ch006

Saade, M. V. (2017). Procedural Remedies as Continuing Violations and Therapeutic Jurisprudence as Best Practice to Prevent Workplace Harassment in the United States. In D. Halder & K. Jaishankar (Eds.), *Therapeutic Jurisprudence and Overcoming Violence Against Women* (pp. 147–170). Hershey, PA: IGI Global. doi:10.4018/978-1-5225-2472-4.ch010

Sánchez-Fernández, M. D., Cardona, J. R., & Martínez-Fernández, V. (2017). Comparative Perspectives on CSR 2.0 in the Contexts of Galicia and North of Portugal. In M. Camilleri (Ed.), *CSR 2.0 and the New Era of Corporate Citizenship* (pp. 165–186). Hershey, PA: IGI Global. doi:10.4018/978-1-5225-1842-6.ch009

Sarter, E. K. (2017). CSR, Public Spending, and the State: The Use of Public Procurement as a Lever to Foster Social Responsibility. In M. Camilleri (Ed.), *CSR 2.0 and the New Era of Corporate Citizenship* (pp. 55–75). Hershey, PA: IGI Global. doi:10.4018/978-1-5225-1842-6.ch004

Schnackenberg, H. L., & Simard, D. A. (2017). *Challenges Facing Female Department Chairs in Contemporary Higher Education: Emerging Research and Opportunities* (pp. 1–90). Hershey, PA: IGI Global. doi:10.4018/978-1-5225-1891-4

Sierotowicz, T. (2015). The Diversification of the Creative Activity of Men and Women in Poland, Hungary, Ireland, and Norway. In S. Moore (Ed.), *Contemporary Global Perspectives on Gender Economics* (pp. 264–292). Hershey, PA: IGI Global. doi:10.4018/978-1-4666-8611-3.ch014

Sikulibo, J. D. (2017). International Criminal Justice and the New Promise of Therapeutic Jurisprudence: Prospects and Challenges in Conflict-Related Sexual Violence Cases. In D. Halder & K. Jaishankar (Eds.), *Therapeutic Jurisprudence and Overcoming Violence Against Women* (pp. 214–247). Hershey, PA: IGI Global. doi:10.4018/978-1-5225-2472-4.ch014

Sitnikov, C. S., Bocean, C., & Tudor, S. (2017). Integrating New Visions of Education Models and CSR 2.0 towards University Social Responsibility (USR). In M. Camilleri (Ed.), *CSR 2.0 and the New Era of Corporate Citizenship* (pp. 251–273). Hershey, PA: IGI Global. doi:10.4018/978-1-5225-1842-6.ch013

Sowad, A. S. (2016). Migration Affecting Masculinities: The Consequences of Migration on the Construction of Masculinities of Migrant Bangladeshi Men Living in the United Kingdom. In N. Mahtab, S. Parker, F. Kabir, T. Haque, A. Sabur, & A. Sowad (Eds.), *Discourse Analysis as a Tool for Understanding Gender Identity, Representation, and Equality* (pp. 50–73). Hershey, PA: IGI Global. doi:10.4018/978-1-5225-0225-8.ch003

Sowad, A. S. (2016). Migration Affecting Masculinities: The Consequences of Migration on the Construction of Masculinities of Migrant Bangladeshi Men Living in the United Kingdom. In N. Mahtab, S. Parker, F. Kabir, T. Haque, A. Sabur, & A. Sowad (Eds.), *Discourse Analysis as a Tool for Understanding Gender Identity, Representation, and Equality* (pp. 50–73). Hershey, PA: IGI Global. doi:10.4018/978-1-5225-0225-8.ch003

Tan, B. U. (2017). Responsible Corporate Behaviors: Drivers of Corporate Responsibility. In M. Camilleri (Ed.), *CSR 2.0 and the New Era of Corporate Citizenship* (pp. 17–36). Hershey, PA: IGI Global. doi:10.4018/978-1-5225-1842-6.ch002

Thakre, A. G. (2017). Sexual Harassment of Women in Workplace in India: An Assessment of Implementation of Preventive Laws and Practicing of Therapeutic Jurisprudence in New Delhi. In D. Halder & K. Jaishankar (Eds.), *Therapeutic Jurisprudence and Overcoming Violence Against Women* (pp. 135–146). Hershey, PA: IGI Global. doi:10.4018/978-1-5225-2472-4.ch009

Torok, R. (2016). The Role of Women from a Social Media Jihad Perspective: Wife or Warrior? In R. English & R. Johns (Eds.), *Gender Considerations in Online Consumption Behavior and Internet Use* (pp. 161–184). Hershey, PA: IGI Global. doi:10.4018/978-1-5225-0010-0.ch011

Tran, B. (2016). Culturally Gendered: The Institutionalization of Men and Masculinities in Society and Corporations. In N. Mahtab, S. Parker, F. Kabir, T. Haque, A. Sabur, & A. Sowad (Eds.), *Discourse Analysis as a Tool for Understanding Gender Identity, Representation, and Equality* (pp. 99–135). Hershey, PA: IGI Global. doi:10.4018/978-1-5225-0225-8.ch006

Tran, B. (2016). Culturally Gendered: The Institutionalization of Men and Masculinities in Society and Corporations. In N. Mahtab, S. Parker, F. Kabir, T. Haque, A. Sabur, & A. Sowad (Eds.), *Discourse Analysis as a Tool for Understanding Gender Identity, Representation, and Equality* (pp. 99–135). Hershey, PA: IGI Global. doi:10.4018/978-1-5225-0225-8.ch006

Ulichny, J., Ambrey, C. L., & Fleming, C. M. (2015). Social Connectedness and the Declining Life Satisfaction of Australian Females. In S. Moore (Ed.), *Contemporary Global Perspectives on Gender Economics* (pp. 188–211). Hershey, PA: IGI Global. doi:10.4018/978-1-4666-8611-3.ch010

Utomo, A. J. (2016). Online Sisterhood: Women, Income Generation, and Online Social Capital in Urban Indonesia. In R. English & R. Johns (Eds.), *Gender Considerations in Online Consumption Behavior and Internet Use* (pp. 208–227). Hershey, PA: IGI Global. doi:10.4018/978-1-5225-0010-0.ch013

van Tonder, C. L. (2015). Windows on Corporate Ethics: The Organisation and Change. In R. Wolf & T. Issa (Eds.), *International Business Ethics and Growth Opportunities* (pp. 43–73). Hershey, PA: IGI Global. doi:10.4018/978-1-4666-7419-6.ch003

Villegas, M., & McGivern, M. H. (2015). Codes of Ethics, Ethical Behavior, and Organizational Culture from the Managerial Approach: A Case Study in the Colombian Banking Industry. *International Journal of Strategic Information Technology and Applications, 6*(1), 42–56. doi:10.4018/IJSITA.2015010104

Walker, L., & Tarutani, C. (2017). Restorative Justice and Violence Against Women in the United States: An Effort to Decrease the Victim-Offender Overlap and Increase Healing. In D. Halder & K. Jaishankar (Eds.), *Therapeutic Jurisprudence and Overcoming Violence Against Women* (pp. 63–84). Hershey, PA: IGI Global. doi:10.4018/978-1-5225-2472-4.ch005

Warmuth, G., & Hanappi-Egger, E. (2014). Professional Socialization in STEM Academia and its Gendered Impact on Creativity and Innovation. In J. Prescott & J. McGurren (Eds.), *Gender Considerations and Influence in the Digital Media and Gaming Industry* (pp. 156–174). Hershey, PA: IGI Global. doi:10.4018/978-1-4666-6142-4.ch008

Williams, J., Sheridan, L., & McLean, P. (2015). Developing Corporate Social Responsibility Projects: An Explorative Empirical Model of Project Development, Processes, and Actor Involvement in Australia. In R. Wolf, T. Issa, & M. Thiel (Eds.), *Empowering Organizations through Corporate Social Responsibility* (pp. 1–28). Hershey, PA: IGI Global. doi:10.4018/978-1-4666-7294-9.ch001

Windsor, D. (2017). Defining Corporate Social Responsibility for Developing and Developed Countries: Comparing Proposed Approaches. In D. Jamali (Ed.), *Comparative Perspectives on Global Corporate Social Responsibility* (pp. 1–27). Hershey, PA: IGI Global. doi:10.4018/978-1-5225-0720-8.ch001

Wisła, R. (2015). Gender and Industrial Creativity in Poland. In S. Moore (Ed.), *Contemporary Global Perspectives on Gender Economics* (pp. 230–243). Hershey, PA: IGI Global. doi:10.4018/978-1-4666-8611-3.ch012

Wolf, R. (2015). Corporate Social Responsibility in the West (U.S. and West Europe) vs. East (China). In R. Wolf, T. Issa, & M. Thiel (Eds.), *Empowering Organizations through Corporate Social Responsibility* (pp. 97–111). Hershey, PA: IGI Global. doi:10.4018/978-1-4666-7294-9.ch005

Wolf, R. (2015). Corporate Social Responsibility: Contribution to All. In R. Wolf, T. Issa, & M. Thiel (Eds.), *Empowering Organizations through Corporate Social Responsibility* (pp. 255–264). Hershey, PA: IGI Global. doi:10.4018/978-1-4666-7294-9.ch013

Wolf, R. (2015). Self-Awareness: A Way to Promote Ethical Management. In R. Wolf & T. Issa (Eds.), *International Business Ethics and Growth Opportunities* (pp. 147–157). Hershey, PA: IGI Global. doi:10.4018/978-1-4666-7419-6.ch007

Wolf, R., & Thiel, M. (2017). CSR in China: The Road to New Sustainable Business Models. In D. Jamali (Ed.), *Comparative Perspectives on Global Corporate Social Responsibility* (pp. 258–275). Hershey, PA: IGI Global. doi:10.4018/978-1-5225-0720-8.ch013

Yajima, N. (2015). Protecting Traditional Knowledge Associated with Genetic Resources by Corporate Social Responsibility. In R. Wolf, T. Issa, & M. Thiel (Eds.), *Empowering Organizations through Corporate Social Responsibility* (pp. 131–150). Hershey, PA: IGI Global. doi:10.4018/978-1-4666-7294-9. ch007

Yang, K. C., & Kang, Y. (2016). Exploring Female Hispanic Consumers' Adoption of Mobile Social Media in the U.S. In R. English & R. Johns (Eds.), *Gender Considerations in Online Consumption Behavior and Internet Use* (pp. 185–207). Hershey, PA: IGI Global. doi:10.4018/978-1-5225-0010-0.ch012

Yap, N. T., & Ground, K. E. (2017). Socially Responsible Mining Corporations: Before (or in Addition to) Doing Good, Do No Harm. In D. Jamali (Ed.), *Comparative Perspectives on Global Corporate Social Responsibility* (pp. 185–207). Hershey, PA: IGI Global. doi:10.4018/978-1-5225-0720-8.ch009

Young, S. B. (2015). Putting Sustainability and Corporate Responsibility at the Center of Capitalism through Better Valuation of Stakeholder Concerns. In R. Wolf, T. Issa, & M. Thiel (Eds.), *Empowering Organizations through Corporate Social Responsibility* (pp. 151–165). Hershey, PA: IGI Global. doi:10.4018/978-1-4666-7294-9.ch008

Zachorowska-Mazurkiewicz, A. (2015). Women in Transition: Institutional Change and Women's Situation in Poland. In S. Moore (Ed.), *Contemporary Global Perspectives on Gender Economics* (pp. 212–229). Hershey, PA: IGI Global. doi:10.4018/978-1-4666-8611-3.ch011

Zachorowska-Mazurkiewicz, A., & Mroczek, K. (2015). Time Allocation and the Life Cycle of Women and Men in Poland. In S. Moore (Ed.), *Contemporary Global Perspectives on Gender Economics* (pp. 293–314). Hershey, PA: IGI Global. doi:10.4018/978-1-4666-8611-3.ch015

Zebregs, A., & Moratis, L. (2017). Serving the Purpose?: Communicating Self-Serving CSR Motives to Increase Credibility. In M. Camilleri (Ed.), *CSR 2.0 and the New Era of Corporate Citizenship* (pp. 187–208). Hershey, PA: IGI Global. doi:10.4018/978-1-5225-1842-6.ch010

Zgheib, P. W. (2015). *Business Ethics and Diversity in the Modern Workplace* (pp. 1–326). Hershey, PA: IGI Global. doi:10.4018/978-1-4666-7254-3

About the Authors

Nattavud Pimpa is an associate professor in management at the College of Management, Mahidol University. Over the last decade, Dr. Pimpa has been working in various educational and research projects in the area of international business and gender equality in Southeast Asia, diversity management in international business, regional leadership and education, and Trade in Southeast Asia. He was the fellow of the 2014 Australia-ASEAN Emerging Program, recipient of various grants on education and trade in Southeast Asia.

Timothy Moore is a program director at the Burmese Border Consortium and an Adjunct Professor at the University of Melbourne. His work spans in the area of global health, refugees in the border of Burma and Thailand, Harm reductions in Southeast Asia, leadership in international health, and human rights.

Index

Ensure Quality Research is Introduced to the Academic Community

Become an IGI Global Reviewer for Authored Book Projects

Premier Reference Source

Emerging GIS Applications for Emergency and Disaster Management

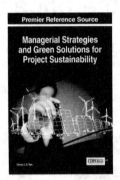

Premier Reference Source

Managerial Strategies and Green Solutions for Project Sustainability

Premier Reference Source

Comparative Approaches to Using R and Python for Statistical Data Analysis

Premier Reference Source

Solutions for High-Touch Communications in a High-Tech World

The overall success of an authored book project is dependent on quality and timely reviews.

In this competitive age of scholarly publishing, constructive and timely feedback significantly expedites the turnaround time of manuscripts from submission to acceptance, allowing the publication and discovery of forward-thinking research at a much more expeditious rate. Several IGI Global authored book projects are currently seeking highly qualified experts in the field to fill vacancies on their respective editorial review boards:

Applications may be sent to:
development@igi-global.com

Applicants must have a doctorate (or an equivalent degree) as well as publishing and reviewing experience. Reviewers are asked to write reviews in a timely, collegial, and constructive manner. All reviewers will begin their role on an ad-hoc basis for a period of one year, and upon successful completion of this term can be considered for full editorial review board status, with the potential for a subsequent promotion to Associate Editor.

If you have a colleague that may be interested in this opportunity, we encourage you to share this information with them.

Information Resources Management Association

Advancing the Concepts & Practices of Information Resources Management in Modern Organizations

Become an IRMA Member

Members of the **Information Resources Management Association (IRMA)** understand the importance of community within their field of study. The Information Resources Management Association is an ideal venue through which professionals, students, and academicians can convene and share the latest industry innovations and scholarly research that is changing the field of information science and technology. Become a member today and enjoy the benefits of membership as well as the opportunity to collaborate and network with fellow experts in the field.

IRMA Membership Benefits:

- **One FREE Journal Subscription**
- **30% Off Additional Journal Subscriptions**
- **20% Off Book Purchases**
- Updates on the latest events and research on Information Resources Management through the IRMA-L listserv.
- Updates on new open access and downloadable content added to Research IRM.
- A copy of the Information Technology Management Newsletter twice a year.
- A certificate of membership.

IRMA Membership $195

Scan code or visit **irma-international.org** and begin by selecting your free journal subscription.

Membership is good for one full year.

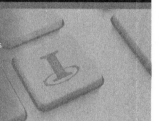